VAPOR 1:
Diary of an Addict
EDUCATION COUNSELOR guide

VIRTUOUS
ADDICTION
PROGRAM
ON RECOVERY

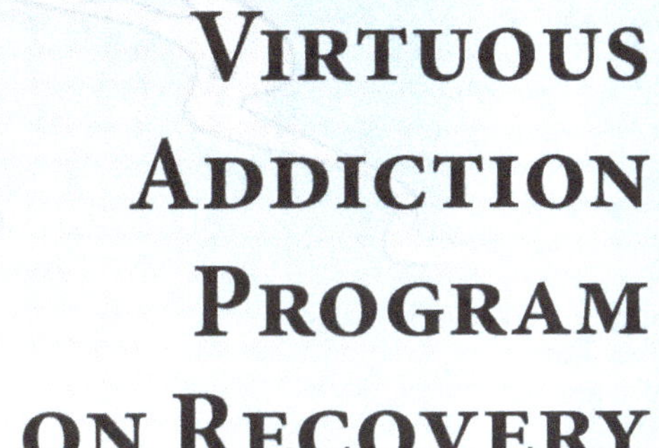

From
Mission
Impossible
Counseling
Services

By:

Lendell L Jones
O.C. Original Counselor

Lendell L Jones

O.C. Original Counselor

Delli Dell & the Dell Family

If Emergency Assistance
is necessary, dial

911

U.S. HOTLINES

Substance Abuse/Prevention..1-800-729-6686

Elder Care Locator...1-800-677-1116

National Child Abuse Hotline..1-800-422-4453

Center for Disease Control and Prevention 1-800-232-4636

Poison Information Center...1-800-222-1222

NAQC (Tobacco Cessation) 1-800-QUIT-NOW

Vapor 1:

Diary of an Addict

Virtuous Addiction Program on Recovery

from Mission Impossible Counseling Services

By

Lendell L Jones

O.C. Original Counselor

Strategies for a Change of Lifestyle

The Counselor's Guide

LEVEL II EDUCATION

Library of Congress Control Number: 2009924146

ISBN: 979-8-88640-983-3 (sc)
ISBN: 979-8-88640-984-0 (hc)
ISBN: 979-8-88640-985-7 (e)

Because of the dynamic nature of the Internet, any web addresses or links contained in this book may have changed since publication and may no longer be valid. The views expressed in this work are solely those of the author and do not necessarily reflect the views of the publisher, and the publisher hereby disclaims any responsibility for them.

For more information or to order additional books, please contact:

Mission Impossible Counseling

4201 Windsor Drive,
Farmington, New Mexico 87401
U.S.A.

505-320-4155

www.missionimpossiblecounseling.com

One Galleria Blvd., Suite 1900, Metairie, LA 70001
1-888-421-2397

Counselors and therapists who use the Vapor 1 Program <u>must complete</u> a Vapor 1 Training Program for education and therapy counseling sessions to be valid. Upon successfully completing the training program, counselors and therapists will receive a certificate of completion.

Introduction - Table of Contents

Education - Table of Contents

INTRODUCTION:
Program Curriculum: Education

Education Table of Contents Continued

In The Back

READ THIS FIRST

Hi! Welcome to the Vapor 1 Program. This short page is here to help you navigate through the Vapor 1 course.

The Vapor 1 Program book is organized into different sections. Each section has different Titles and colored header bars.

Green = Preface–Introduction to the Vapor 1 Program

Blue = Counselor's Orientation

Gold = Educational Tools

Orange = Participant's Orientation

Grey = Education Section

Blue = Education Forms

Red = Laws

We've done this to try and make it easier to navigate this book. You'll notice this page has a green header and footer bar so it's part of the Preface section.

We don't believe that counseling success is based on chance. It's based on facts and doing what works. We want to continue to make this program better and more successful for you. And we need your help to do this. On our website, http://MissionImpossibleCounseling.com, we have placed a survey for counselors and participants. We ask that you go online and fill out the short survey. It will only take a couple of minutes. This will provide us feedback to help make this program better for everyone.

Thanks,

The Vapor 1 Team

SECTION OF THE BOOK YOU'RE IN

DON'T FORGET THAT COLOR INDICATES THE SECTION!

THIS IS DELLI DELL, OUR ENTERTAINING CARTOON HOST. YOU'LL FOLLOW DELLI THROUGH HIS MANY ADVENTURES IN THE BOOK. EVEN THOUGH WE DEAL WITH SOME HEAVY AND SERIOUS TOPICS, DELLI HELPS US LIGHTEN THE MOOD A LITTLE.

Dedication & Acknowledgement

I am the third generation of men in my family who has been deeply affected by alcohol/drug addiction and maladaptive behavior. For me, it began when I was ten years old. My grandfather ran a gambling shack and a bootlegger house. I note this because throughout this program I will reflect on what I experienced that brought me to where I am today. I wrote, "Diary of an Addict," to share with others what helped me to alleviate some of the suffering I experienced as a child that I too carried on into my adulthood. I am very aware that many of the participants that this program treats may have vastly worst histories than what I address in this book. My gratification comes from the possibility that I can transform my personal history into something that can help others. If I could reverse time, my wish would be to discover a way for my family and me not to have suffered because of addiction and maladaptive behavior, but I did, and we did for so many heart-wrenching years.

I feel very fortunate to have been given the opportunity to develop Vapor 1. I am very eager about the development phase and the progress this program has had in so many people's lives. It is quite remarkable to think how young this program is and the effect that it is having in the addiction and behavioral field.

Within the Vapor 1 program, I have articulated a model of treatment that will help others reach their potential in life. Note: up to date, no program has all the answers or solutions for addiction and maladaptive behavior. I am aware that there is no easy answer. I recognize also that Vapor 1 is a structured program that invites participants to address treatment issues. Vapor 1 incorporates a personalized, unique format with a large number of worksheets and other treatment strategies that will bring participants closer to finding the answers they're seeking.

Vapor 1 is based on one's own coping strategies. This program is action-oriented and informational, along with being sensitive to the emotional pain that brings people into treatment. I have designed this program to take a sympathetic attitude and to be sincere in the techniques that are used. I know from personal experience that changing maladaptive behaviors is not easy. It takes practice and refinement, but the rewards are well worth the effort.

Vapor 1 has evolved over the years. In earlier years, I tended to do board discussions and send participants home with homework to be completed by the next session. I discovered during this time that assignments were coming back to be processed with half-hearted effort. Therefore, I put a great deal of thought and energy into devising a various task program. I focused on inventing clever, witty, and creative ways to present tasks to participants.

I am respectfully aware that change remains a mystery for most people. No one knows who will or will not succeed in treatment. However, one thing is clear: for success to happen, the process requires the participant and the therapist to put their best effort into motion. The Vapor

1 program is only a tool, and like any tool, it can be used to help only when the participant is willing to put forth the effort. I did not design Vapor 1 with the expectation that it would work for everyone. On any given day, a participant might say, "the Vapor 1 program doesn't work for me" and that may be a truth for them. I designed Vapor 1 to help people move into a position that allows them to start working for themselves. However, optimistic participants who demonstrate a desire to work will usually come away from treatment with a renewed sense of hope and a new feeling of power over their addiction and behavior.

I graciously acknowledge Mission Impossible Counseling and the Impossible Crew who have been so gracious with their time and provided thoughtful comments and very useful suggestions in support of this project.

A recognition shout-out to Mark G. Mishek and Hazelden Publishing. In 1990 when I picked up and read my first Hazelden magazine, I have ever since been inspired to search deeper into the field of addiction and behavior. Throughout the years, the friendly and professional staff of Hazelden has supported, encouraged, and challenged me to do better as an author and provider.

I have learned through life's hard knocks and experienced the blessing of having a great graphic designer on the team, and I don't think I could have chosen a more suitable graphic designer and idealist for this project than my dear friend Daniel Arnold. I am very grateful for Daniel who has been with me from the beginning (tough hard beginnings, please believe me) while providing sound advice, encouragement, and support. Every artist must know that finalizing any production can be the most challenging time for any project. Although, through uncertain moments and challenges, Daniel was assuring, guiding, and always asked the right questions to help this project succeed. I have learned much from Daniel and I am very appreciative of his talents and wisdom. If God be willing and the creek doesn't rise Mission Impossible Counseling, the Impossible Crew and I, are looking forward to collaborating with Daniel on upcoming projects.

Chief Business Advisor of this project thanks be to Larry Armstrong. Mr. Armstrong has been my business advisor since the birth of Mission Impossible Counseling. I thank God for putting such a spiritual person in my life that has helped me mature in life and in business.

A special appreciation goes out to my beautiful bride Kala and my two wonderful children Shylisa and Brendon Jones. I can't thank you all enough for your patience with me as I sacrificed many hours of family time in the studio to bring this project to life.

Above all, I acknowledge my Lord and Savior Jesus Christ for blessing me with the ability to go through with this project.

People of note who helped make this book possible:

My parents:

- Leonard and Mozell Elliott Jones

My Aunts and Uncle:

- Precious Robbinson
- Jeweline Johnson
- Willie Phillip

My Siblings:

- Alice Mitchell
- Raymond Elliott
- Debbie Locket
- Sharon Lucero
- Beverly Jones
- Sonji LaFonda Jones

My mother-in-law, brothers and sister-in-law:

- Sharon Steinle
- Alan and Elaine Steinle
- Dale Lockett
- Edward Reese
- Thomas Rollison
- Jessie Elliott

The Impossible Crew:

- Daniel Arnold
- Brittany Page
- Jeramiah Townsend
- Larry Armstrong
- Neil Johnson

To all the people and families who are suffering, with complete compassion, I dedicate this book to you.

To all therapists out there sincerely working hard to help improve someone's life, I dedicate this book to you.

To all my friends, I dedicate this book to you and thank you for being a friend and not bailing out on me when things got tough.

To all the clinicians who have helped and supported me throughout my career and shown favor to the Vapor 1 project, I dedicate this book to you.

Welcome

I am pleased to announce that you have now joined the proud ranks of the counselors of Vapor 1 programs. This life-changing accomplishment prepares you to join your fellow Vapor 1 alumni who have made the decision to become positive family and community leaders. Most importantly, it prepares you for a productive future in which you will make many contributions to the lives of others.

Vapor 1 at Mission Impossible Counseling is dedicated to excellence in professional addiction and behavioral counseling. At Mission Impossible Counseling, the staff is committed to promoting character development and building a vibrant intellectual community that serves the highest and best interests of all community members.

Vapor 1 is well recognized for delivering first-rate education and therapy in our accredited programs to those interested in extraordinary quality and affordable cost. Our programs are designed for participants from a wide variety of backgrounds. The core curricula in our programs emphasize functional skills in public and private culture. In addition to the core, participants gain advanced knowledge in salient perspectives such as managing diversity, innovation, responding to changing environments, team building, social issues management, and Global Assessment of Functioning (GAF) identity.

Participants will be challenged to confront their own strengths and weaknesses and seek new ways to improve their personal effectiveness in society.

The Vapor 1 program is a challenging and rewarding experience specially designed for participants who are interested in changing their lifestyle.

Mission

We seek to develop and inform family, community, and world leaders through a balance of teaching, counseling, and therapeutic interventions, and to contribute to society's development and the quality of life of our participants.

Vision

We envision a nationally recognized Vapor 1 program that will build on Mission Impossible Counseling's strategic curriculum to provide high-quality education and therapy to help participants enhance and recognize their skills and abilities.

Goals

We aim to provide high-quality; value-added programs that foster a vibrant climate of addiction and behavioral counseling excellence that actively engages many elements that strengthen the home and community. We aim to promote preparedness and readiness to work with a diverse population.

We give you our sincere appreciation for checking us out. Enjoy your journey!

A Street Counselor. . .

A **Street Counselor** is the way one lives his/her life. Going out on the **street**s or wherever, kicking flavor about what is really happening(concerning the reality of addiction and maladaptive behavior), and shutting down all alibis and excuses while working hard daily to make a difference in someone's life.

A **Street Counselor** is not lazy; he/she is consistently out there learning about the community's needs. He/she gets results by using his/her smarts about the addiction/maladaptive community.

A **Street Counselor** has ambition and a serious approach to life. He/she is mature, and doesn't necessarily approach the addiction/maladaptive community traditionally textbook-style. A **Street Counselor** can apply to any race, and it is the way you uphold and carry yourself.

Special thanks to everyone who has supported Mission Impossible Counseling throughout the years in the hood and counting. My intent has always been to bring **street counseling** to the surface worldwide. Much love to all the street counselors who have been working with the population of people in all the hoods, projects, prisons, ghettos, and reservations throughout the world. You are dearly appreciated. Eternal love to my inner circle of friends and family who really know what I go through and work to keep me focused and healthy.

Peace and love to all the young **street counselors** who are coming up and have the desire to make a difference in their community and the world.

Street Counselors are professional, ethical, and credential-qualified counselors by state licensing boards' standards.

I am truly grateful to all therapists who have contributed to the field of addiction and behavior and who have helped me develop as I learn about a **real Street Counselor.**

Street Counselor Up....

> *"The game is real, it ain't how much you say, it's what you say and how you're representing yo mouth (verb is the word you gotta move somethin'). People are dying every day from this sickness called addiction, so please believe me. I am a true blue street counselor and I got no time to play."*

-Lendell L Jones

NAADAC Code of Ethics

Introduction

NAADAC recognizes that its members and NCC certified counselors live and work in many diverse communities. The NAADAC Code of Ethics was written to govern the conduct of its members and it is the accepted standard of conduct for addiction counselors certified by the National Certification Commission.

I. The Counseling Relationship

It is the responsibility of the addiction professional to safeguard the integrity of the counseling relationship and to ensure that the participant is provided with beneficial services. The participant will be provided access to effective treatment and referral giving consideration to individual educational, legal and financial needs. Addiction Professionals also recognize their responsibility to the larger society and any specific legal obligations that may, on limited occasions, supersede loyalty to participants.

The addiction professional shall provide the participant and/or guardian with accurate and complete information regarding the extent of the professional relationship. In all areas of function, the addiction professional is likely to encounter individuals who are vulnerable and exploitable. In such relationships he or she seeks to nurture and support the development of a relationship of equals rather than to take unfair advantage. In personal relationships, the addiction professional seeks to foster self-sufficiency and healthy self-esteem in others. In relationships with participants he or she provides only that level and length of care that is necessary and acceptable.

II. Evaluation, Assessment and Interpretation of Participant Data

The addiction professional uses assessment instruments as one component of the counseling/ treatment and referral process taking into account the participant's personal and cultural background. The assessment process promotes the well-being of individual participants or groups. Addiction professionals base their recommendations/reports on approved evaluation instruments and procedures. The designated assessment instruments are ones for which reliability has been verified by research.

III. Confidentiality/Privileged Communication and Privacy

Addiction professionals shall provide information to participants regarding confidentiality and any reasons for releasing information in adherence with confidentiality laws. When providing

services to families, couples or groups, the limits and exceptions to confidentiality must be reviewed and a written document describing confidentiality must be provided to each person. Once private information is obtained by the addiction professional, standards of confidentiality apply. Confidential information is disclosed when appropriate with valid consent from a participant or guardian. Every effort is made to protect the confidentiality of participant information, and in very specific cases or situations to disclose information appropriately and according to federal law.

IV. Professional Responsibility

The addiction professional espouses objectivity and integrity and maintains the highest standards in the services provided. The addiction professional recognizes that effectiveness in his or her profession is based on the ability to be worthy of trust. The professional has taken time to reflect on the ethical implications of clinical decisions and behavior using competent authority as a guide. Further, the addiction professional recognizes that those who assume the role of assisting others to live a more responsible life take on the ethical accountability of living responsibly. The addiction professional recognizes that even in a life well-lived, harm might be done to others by words and actions. When he or she becomes aware that any work or action has done harm, he or she admits the error and does what is possible to repair or ameliorate the harm except when to do so would cause greater harm. Professionals recognize the many ways in which they influence participants and others within the community and take this fact into consideration as they make decisions in their personal conduct.

V. Working in a Culturally Diverse World

An Addiction professional understands the significance of the role that ethnicity and culture plays in an individual's perceptions and how he or she lives in the world. Addiction professionals shall remain aware that many individuals have disabilities which may or may not be obvious. Some disabilities are invisible and unless described might not appear to inhibit expected social, work and healthcare interactions. Included in the invisible disabled category are those persons who are hearing impaired, have a learning disability, have a history of brain or physical injuries and those affected by chronic illness. Persons having such limitations might be younger than age 65. Part of the intake and assessment must then include a question about any additional factor that must be considered when working with the participant.

VI. Workplace Standards

The addiction professional recognizes that the profession is founded on national standards of competency which promote the best interests of society, the participant, the individual addiction professional and the profession as a whole. The addiction professional recognizes the need for ongoing education as a component of professional competency and development.

VII. Supervision and Consultation

Addiction professionals who supervise others accept the obligation to facilitate further professional development of these individuals by providing accurate and current information, timely evaluations and constructive consultation. Counseling supervisors are aware of the power differential in their relationships with supervisees and take precautions to maintain ethical standards. In relationships with students, employees and supervisees he/she strives to develop full creative potential and mature independent functioning.

VIII. Resolving Ethical Issues

The addiction professional shall behave in accordance with legal, ethical and moral standards for his or her work. To this end, professionals will attempt to resolve ethical dilemmas with direct and open communication among all parties involved and seek supervision and/or consultation as appropriate.

IX. Communication and Published Works

The addiction professional who submits for publication or prepares handouts for participants, students or for general distribution shall be aware of and adhere to copyright laws.

X. Policy and Political Involvement

The addiction professional is strongly encouraged to the best of his or her ability, to actively engage the legislative processes, educational institutions and the general public to change public policy and legislation to make possible opportunities and choice of service for all human beings of any ethnic or social background whose lives are impaired by alcoholism and drug abuse.

Please use this resource and share it with your colleagues.

For more information contact naadac@naadac.org or 800.548.0497.

Vapor 1 Presents . . .

Level II Education

This is the educational (information) part in the participant workbook. Much of this section will be lectures and board discussions. Participants are invited to take notes and ask questions. Participants will have the opportunity to understand that positive and negative outcomes are determined by the choices one makes.

Participants are required to do a check-in and feeling journal report at the beginning of each educational group.

THE BASICS

Structurally, there are two completely different parts to the Vapor 1 counseling presentation: composition and delivery.

1. **Composition** - creating, organizing, formatting, and structuring ideas, information, insights, and imagery. It is hard work and hard thinking. Participants may have different personalities and value systems. It is critical to be able to think fast and recognize participants' facial, body, and vocal language.

2. **Delivery** - presentation is an attitude, mindset, vision, and problem-solving stage performance. It is hard work and hard thinking, and should include teaching, coaching, encouragement, and entertainment if possible.

Note: At the beginning of each Education chapter, you will find a page titled *"A Question for the Provider."*

These questions are to help you think through each chapter before going through it with participants. Study the chapters before facilitating the sessions with the participants. Answer the questions with full explanations on the questions for the provider page. Become familiar with your own transparency on the topic being discussed. If you are not comfortable presenting the material, seek or ask a co-worker to facilitate the session. In the note column, make sure to write down any information you may feel or think is important and appropriate to share. Self-disclosure by a counselor can be used to build bridges with participants; HOWEVER, it can also be dangerous to disclose personal information to participants. Remember, self-disclosing any information with participants should be planned and strategized, and with a justifiable reason.

On the bottom of the "A Question for Providers" page, if you haven't found closure on a past or present event pertaining to the chapter, write your plan on how you will find closure.

Because of these individual notes, it is CRUCIAL that all providers have their own counselor's guidebook.

Healthy Affirmations

(According to Lendell L Jones)

This is Lendell's belief system. No other person/people is mandated to follow this system:

1. Trust God, pray, and study his word daily.

2. Thank God daily.

3. Respect yourself and others daily.

4. Study to improve your knowledge daily.

5. Work to improve a talent or skill daily.

6. Be fair when dealing with others daily.

7. Exercise daily.

8. Eat something healthy daily (It's okay to have junk food sometimes).

9. Drink water daily.

10. Take care of your appearance daily.

11. Ask God for forgiveness daily (We all make mistakes).

12. Be faithful to your mate daily (When temptation appears, ask God for help).

13. Think of ways to improve your relationship daily.

14. Be faithful in paying it forward.

15. Help somebody with something daily.

16. Speak positively about yourself and another person daily.

17. Tell someone you love them daily.

18. Be strong and fair. Be a leader to your kids daily.

19. Be strong and fair. Be a leader or co-leader to your spouse daily.

20. Express your gratitude to someone daily.

STAGES TO RECOVERY

Stage One: Precontemplation

In this stage, participants are not thinking seriously about changing and are not interested in receiving help. Participants in this stage tend to defend their usage/behaviors and do not feel it is a problem.

Suggestion:
Be watchful of participants with the tan chair during groups or
individual sessions.

Stage Two: Contemplation

In this stage, participants are aware of the personal consequences of their usage/behaviors and may spend time thinking about their issues. Although they are able to consider the possibility of change, they tend to be ambivalent about it.

Suggestion:
Be watchful of participants with the gray chair during groups or individual
sessions.

Stage Three: Preparation/Determination

In this stage, participants have made a commitment to making a change. Their motivation for change is reflected by statements such as: "This is serious, I've got to change my lifestyle," or "What can I do to change?"

Suggestion:
Be watchful of participants with the brown chair during groups
or individual sessions.

Stage Four: Action

In this stage, participants believe they have the ability to change their behaviors and are actively involved in taking steps to change their usage/behaviors by using a variety of different techniques.

Suggestion: Be watchful of participants with the blue chair during groups
and individual sessions.

Vapor 1 Description

The Vapor 1 program will go beyond the typical overview of the stages of behavioral change, focusing also on the processes, markers, and context that play a vital role in the participant's recovery. Matching appropriate interventions to the participant's stage of change will be crucial. The Vapor 1 approach will be applied to the participant's desire to have a change of lifestyle, allowing counselors to practice creating collaborative interventions that can be used in treatment planning. By counselors truly understanding their own confidence level and skills of delivery that allow them to focus on the decision-making of the participant, this will help them be able to apply all aspects of the Vapor 1 model to their work with participants.

Vapor 1 Philosophy

Participants are sometimes put into a position that reflects: "I must abstain from drinking/using and maladaptive behaviors, or else." Although the current situation may stick out like a sore thumb, many times there are many limitations in one's life other than the issue that brought them into their current undesirable situations. Vapor 1 approaches and reviews many areas in one's life other than the sore thumb (current situation). By helping participants to view their complete selves and other possible problem areas, it may increase the awareness of the question that so many ask themselves silently: "Now what?" "Okay, I am not drinking/using/doing the behavior that brought me here. But where do I go from here?" By allowing participants to focus on and address as many troubled areas as possible in their own lives, it can increase their intimate connection of identity with self. The "now what?" question often turns into, "now what area in my life is important enough for me to strengthen?" When participants begin to look at all the concerned areas in their lives (conscious or subconscious) this can increase their desire to address current situations more openly and honestly.

Vapor 1 Providers

The first step to becoming an advanced skilled Vapor 1 provider is to get to know your community. You already have a love for and loyalty to your community. That's understandable and commendable. But are you knowledgeable? Do you really know the status of your community? You must get to know your community if you are to know the kind of participants you will be working with. So, begin by making a realistic assessment of both your skills and your community. Don't let your love for complacency blind you to the facts. Be as honest and as fair as you can about your community's needs.

No greater honor and no graver responsibility can come to a person who chooses to help strengthen others. The choice you make to be a Vapor 1 provider will likely have much to do with the future, spirit, and effectiveness of your community as anything you can do. To do your work right will demand your highest and best effort.

Adopt the procedure you will follow:

1. Study your community.

2. Develop a profile of your community's needs.

3. Know your leadership style.

4. Commit to a daily work schedule.

5. Be well prepared.

All this involves time and work, but it will be time well spent. A little sweat now may save you from a lot of tears later.

Questions you may ask yourself:

1. What conversions led me to want to be a counselor and called to this career?

2. What are my natural or spiritual gifts that make me effective in this work?

3. What is my involvement in the community?

4. Do I have the support of my family?

5. What are my ultimate goals in life?

6. Who are my clinical role models?

7. What is my understanding of theories, models, and of reality?

8. What new programs have I inaugurated?

9. How do I deal with conflict?

10. Have I grown clinically in the past two years?

There is an intangible to counseling that I call "heart." Heart is hard to define, but when it's present, you recognize it. It is the power to move an audience. It is a message that comes from your heart to your participant's heart. It moves you and them, into action.

A Vapor 1 counselor is a shepherd. One who is among the flock, feeding it, and bleeding for it. This necessitates a special love and temperament. There is a well-worn saying, "People don't care how much you know until they know how much you care."

If at any point you decide you are not a Vapor 1 counselor, stop using the program immediately. Don't keep hanging around, going through the motions.

Remember This: Devotional character is the essence that makes a Vapor 1 counselor shine and naturally, most people are attracted to the light.

Communities must change in order to prosper and communities change because people change. Nothing changes until something starts.

Counselors be Real

Every coach that coaches basketball knows that every kid is not going to be a Michael Jordan, Magic Johnson, Larry Bird, or Dirk Nowitzki. These elite basketball players are the ones who have the heart, the desire, and the skills to win. This formula is the same ingredient for your participants. However, as a counselor, your job is to work with all participants, regardless of their dedication, and to have the ability to meet them where they are in life. (Sounds tough, it is). Counseling is a high-intensity job. To truly be effective, counselors need to be physically, emotionally, mentally, and spiritually rested.

Counselors be Real

Every **trainer** that **trains** boxers knows that every kid is not going to be a Muhammad Ali, Sugar Ray Leonard, Oscar De La Hoya, or Jack Dempsey. These elite boxers are the ones who have the heart, the desire, and the skills to win. This formula is the same ingredient for therapists. Having a Doctorate, Ph.D., MA, BA, certification, license, who may be in recovery themselves, or has any other title does not necessarily qualify them as a good therapist. However, all these things can be positive objectives along the way, as participants identify their goals.

Typically counselors and therapists will work with three types of participants.

Participant 1
I have not identified a problem with how I am living. Therefore I don't see a need to adjust my lifestyle. (Conscious or subconscious)

Participant 2
I have identified a problem with how I am living. Yet I don't have the courage, desire, or intelligence to adjust my lifestyle. (Conscious or subconscious)

Participant 3
 I have identified a problem with how I am living. And I have the courage, desire, and intelligence to adjust my lifestyle. (Conscious or subconscious)

Vapor 1 was designed to be counselor and therapist-friendly! Stay on task and present materials confidently to all participants. Please stop beating yourself up; you do not have the power or magic to change anyone. Ultimately the participants decide what they want out of life. Your job is to always be professional, ethical, and knowledgeable while facilitating this program.

Vapor 1 - Participant Questioner

Have you or anyone you know ever been involved in a domestic violence dispute?...................
.... Yes☐...No☐

Have you or anyone you know ever driven under the influence of alcohol or drugs
 more than five times?.. Yes☐...No☐

Have you or anyone you know ever experienced physical problems due to alcohol use?............
.... Yes☐...No☐

Have you or anyone you know ever experienced legal or family problems due to
drug use other than alcohol? .... Yes☐...No☐

Do you or anyone you know have low self-esteem? .... Yes☐...No☐

Do you or anyone you know have a hard time communicating or getting along
with a significant other for a long period of time?.. Yes☐...No☐

Have you or anyone you know had anger episodes which led to embarrassing feelings? ....
.... Yes☐...No☐

Do you or anyone you know need to improve with parenting skills? .... Yes☐...No☐

Do you or anyone you know live with a disability? .... Yes☐...No☐

Have you or anyone you know ever relapsed back to alcohol or drug use? .... Yes☐...No☐

Have you or anyone you know ever committed more than one crime? .... Yes☐...No☐

Have you or anyone you know lost more money than intended by gambling? ...... Yes☐...No☐

Do you or anyone you know fail to exercise on a regular basis? .... Yes☐...No☐

Have you or anyone you know stayed in an unhealthy relationship? .... Yes☐...No☐

Are you or anyone you know afraid of your anger? .... Yes☐...No☐

Have you or anyone you know ever been involved with pornography? .... Yes☐...No☐

Have you or anyone you know attempted or committed suicide? .... Yes☐...No☐

If you answered yes to any of the questions above, this program may be for you. These topics and many more will be addressed as you continue to work through the Vapor 1 program.

Intro to the LSSA: Lendell's Strength Screening Assessment

(The LSSA)

The chart below identifies strengths by targeting specific areas. Circle the number that best describes your strength (how strong do you think you are at managing and coping with the specific area in your life within the last six months). 1 is low strength and 10 is high strength. Then complete the feelings statements.

The LSSA is designed in two parts:

1. **Cognitive** - the mental process. "I think I'm this strong in a particular area."

2. **Emotional** - the feeling process. "I feel this way about a particular area."

Counselors should look for incongruence in how the participant thinks and feels. Be mindful when presenting this tool. Counselors should express the importance of writing complete sentences as explanations when completing the feeling part.

By using one or two words with no explanation, it makes it hard to make an accurate suggestion of how connected the participant's thinking is with his/her feeling.

When probing is necessary, ask the participant if they think the total strength score is accurate and why they feel so.

Throughout the course, it is suggested that counselors and participants reflect back on the LSSA and identify any progress or regression.

Challenge participants to evaluate themselves and their condition throughout the course.

How?

Ask participants direct questions such as, what's the purpose of them being here in counseling?

Counselors note: When participants' response contradicts the reality of a specific condition, challenge the purpose. This is called problem marking. Remember, challenging doesn't mean confrontation.

Let participants know all <u>do</u> behaviors have a purpose. The cycle will always be:

1. The event

2. How does one think about the event

3. How does one feel about the event

4. What does one <u>do</u> about the event

The dynamics of the cycle will either be a successful (positive) or a failure (negative) outcome.

Outcomes are determined by 3 traits:

1. **Character**
    Values and belief

2. **Self-esteem**
    Self-image or feelings about self

3. **Courage**
    Confident to continue while knowing the risk

A reality approach is seen in the movie "Rudy." Rudy might have the will to start for the Notre Dame Fighting Irish, but reality says he does not have the capability to be a starter for the team.

The sooner participants understand that the heart, mind, and ability must equally yoke, the sooner they may place themselves in a position to begin their purpose in life.

Lendell's Strength Screening Assessment

LSSA - Part 1

The chart below identifies strengths by targeting specific areas. Circle the number that best describes your strength (how strong do you think you are at managing and coping with the specific area in your life within the last six months). 1 is low strength and 10 is high strength.

School/Work ....LOW 1____2____3____4____5____6____7____8____9____10 HIGH

Obeying Laws/Rules LOW 1____2____3____4____5____6____7____8____9____10 HIGH

Self-Esteem ....LOW 1____2____3____4____5____6____7____8____9____10 HIGH

Past Hurt ....LOW 1____2____3____4____5____6____7____8____9____10 HIGH

Present Hurt ....LOW 1____2____3____4____5____6____7____8____9____10 HIGH

Unresolved Anger ....LOW 1____2____3____4____5____6____7____8____9____10 HIGH

Current Anger ....LOW 1____2____3____4____5____6____7____8____9____10 HIGH

Family Relationships LOW 1____2____3____4____5____6____7____8____9____10 HIGH

Physical Pain ....LOW 1____2____3____4____5____6____7____8____9____10 HIGH

Eating Healthy ....LOW 1____2____3____4____5____6____7____8____9____10 HIGH

Physically Healthy .....LOW 1____2____3____4____5____6____7____8____9____10 HIGH

Completing Goals .....LOW 1____2____3____4____5____6____7____8____9____10 HIGH

Expressing Feelings .LOW 1____2____3____4____5____6____7____8____9____10 HIGH

Lendell L Jones

O.C. Original Counselor

LSSA - Part 2

At school/work, I feel _______________________________________

____

____

Following laws and rules makes me feel _______________________

____

____

My self-esteem at this time makes me feel _____________________

____

____

My past hurt makes me feel ___________________________________

____

____

My present hurt makes me feel ________________________________

____

____

My unresolved anger makes me feel ___________________________

____

____

My current anger makes me feel ______________________________

____

____

My family relationship makes me feel _________________________

____

____

My physical pain makes me feel _______________________________

____

____

My ability to eat healthy makes me feel _______________________

____

____

My taking care of my body or not taking care of my body makes me feel _______________

____

____

My ability to accomplish goals makes me feel __________________

____

____

My ability to share true feelings with others makes me feel _____________

____

____

Add all circled numbers to determine overall strength: Total: ____________

If total points are: 13 to 42 = Low overall strength

43 to 86 = Moderate overall strength

87 to 130 = High overall strength

CHAIR THERAPY

Modern science teaches that evolution and transformation can arise out of chaos. This is good information to chew on. By understanding that the chaos theory is another way to identify how much growth is occurring, observe closely as participants continue to reveal their own self-assessment of how they are doing.

Each group and individual session will have four different-colored chairs available for participants to choose from. Counselors will clearly explain the choosing of chair patterns to participants.

1. By choosing a tan chair the participant is communicating that they don't at all feel counseling is helping them in their everyday life.

2. By choosing a grey chair the participant is communicating that they slightly feel that counseling is helping them in their everyday life.

3. By choosing a brown chair the participant is communicating that they moderately feel that counseling is helping them in their everyday life.

4. By choosing a blue chair the participant is communicating that they strongly feel that counseling is helping them in their everyday life.

Be encouraging to participants while letting them know it's okay to feel how they feel and that there is no right or wrong way to feel. It is crucial that counselors do not target any chair group or change the flow or structure of Composition and Delivery during sessions.

However, it is important for counselors to keep note of the chair pattern as participants go through the program for it may be helpful when identifying stages of change.

The Formula - *I'm as good as I am*

Write on the board if you have one or improvise with this exercise "I'm as good as I am" and ask participants to assess and internalize the ten statements below:

1. Being a responsible parent (poor, fair, good)

2. Being responsible for your family's needs (poor, fair, good)

3. Being responsible for your own needs (poor, fair, good)

4. Being honest with others (poor, fair, good)

5. Being honest with self (poor, fair, good)

6. Being responsible and doing your best at work (poor, fair, good)

7. Being responsible and doing your best trying to find work (poor, fair, good)

8. Being responsible by working to improve your education (poor, fair, good)

9. Being responsible and following through on what you say you will do (poor, fair, good)

10. Being responsible by following the rules and laws of society (poor, fair, good)

Ask participants, overall how responsible are you on the scale? poor 1,2,3,4,5,6,7,8,9,10 good

Remind participants that their character really does count! How you are living, tells your story. It's not about what you say you are doing, but what you are doing.

Note:

Counselors, you must be able to adapt skills that will allow the participants to understand how they are living and how that correlates with their own interpretation of responsibilities.

Note: This exercise is recommended to be used randomly throughout the course at the beginning of counseling sessions. As counselors notice changes in participants' self-reports, they may ask participants to elaborate on the changes.

Lendell L Jones   O.C. Original Counselor

Check-In

How are you feeling today? _________________ Why? _________________________________

____

What coping skills did you use last week? ____

____

Did you use any alcohol or drugs last week? __________ If yes, explain: ____________________

____

What commitment did you follow through with last week? ________________________________

____

What commitment did you not follow through with last week? _____________________________

____

Check-Out

Share one thing you learned from your check-in: ____

____

What is your new commitment? ____

____

Who will you contact if you have a hard time coping with a difficult situation? _______________

__________________ Why him/her? ____

____

What was the last thing you accomplished that entitled you to feel good? ____________________

____

What are two positive things you can do for yourself and your family this week? ______________

____

Tracking your thinking and behaviors around drinking, using, and driving

Circle either True or False.

	Mon.	Tues.	Wed.	Thurs.	Fri.	Sat.	Sun.
I thought about drinking or using today	True or False	True or False	True or False	True or False	True or False	True or False	True or False
I was around alcohol/drugs	True or False	True or False	True or False	True or False	True or False	True or False	True or False
I did drink or use	True or False	True or False	True or False	True or False	True or False	True or False	True or False
I thought about drinking or using while driving	True or False	True or False	True or False	True or False	True or False	True or False	True or False
I did drink or use while driving	True or False	True or False	True or False	True or False	True or False	True or False	True or False

What triggers or prevention skills did you experience? _______________________

____

____

____

____

Lendell L Jones

O.C. Original Counselor

FEEDBACK/PROGRESS NOTE

Participant Name: ____

Session Date: ____________________________ Session #: _____________________________

Length of Session: ____________________ Topic: ________________________________

Participant Feedback:

What did you learn? ____

____

How do you feel about today's group? _______________________________

____

Participant view:

Data: (self-report, observations, current issues/stressors, functional impairment, interpersonal behavior, motivation) ____

____

Assessment: (progress, evaluation of intervention, obstacles or barriers) ________________

____

Plan: (tasks to be completed between sessions, objectives for next session, changes, recommendations, date of next session, plan for discharge) _______________________

____

____

Prognosis: How do you think did you do in today's group? Poor? Fair? Good? Why? _________

____

____

____

Vapor 1 Education Course Discharge Report

Organization Reporting to: ____

____

Participant: ____

Participant ID or alternate ID: ____________________________

Date: __________________

Agency: ______________________________   Counselor: ______________________________

Section 1: Awareness and Ability

Chapter ______ %__________   Chapter ______ %__________

Chapter ______ %__________   Chapter ______ %__________

Chapter ______ %__________   Chapter ______ %__________

Chapter ______ %__________   Chapter ______ %__________

Chapter ______ %__________   Chapter ______ %__________

Test Score Average: ____________

Section 2: Program Participation

Participants education course participation rating %: (circle one)

<----   0,   10,   20,   30,   40,   50,   60,   70,   80,   90,   100   --->%

Section 3: Program Attendance

Participants attendance: 4+ absences 60%..........1-3 absences 80%..........0 absences 100%

Attended Hours__________ Attended Weeks ____________ Elapsed Weeks __________

Section 4: Outside Program Attendance

Participants (total weeks______) support group's attendance while in the program

0 meetings, 50%_____   1 meeting weekly, 80%_____   2+ meetings weekly, 100%_____

Section 5: Counselor Judgment

Counselor Prognosis: Poor   Fair   Good

Counselor Notes:

____

____

____

____

____

Counselor Recommendations:

____

____

____

____

____

____

______________________________________   ______________________

Counselor Signature   Date

Vapor 1 - Participant Orientation

Vapor 1 theory is residential treatment may not always be the primary or best solution for people with addiction or maladaptive behaviors. (However, sometimes residential treatment is necessary.)

Vapor 1 believes that most people will do well in residential treatment. Re-entry back into familiar surroundings is where relapse often begins.

Vapor 1 subscribes to the Sociocultural treatment modalities that include the community reinforcement approach, therapeutic communities, motivational techniques, contingency management, optional culturally specific interventions, relapse prevention techniques, advocates for 12-step programs when the need fits, and Rational Recovery.

Vapor 1 focus is on making sure each participant has the best solution offered for their unique clinical needs.

Vapor 1 groups utilize a mix of Community Reinforcement Approaches and Moral Recognition Therapies. All ASAM standards are adhered to with each group and have not more than 12 participants without a co-facilitator.

Vapor 1 realizes that nationwide, some experts believe that the success rate for the number of participants that do any type of treatment, inpatient or outpatient is below 8% for those that go on to maintain long-term sobriety.

Vapor 1 chooses to be real about the recovery success rate. Our program is dedicated to bring this percentage up. The idea is to shut down all alibis and excuses that participants, family members, and communities have become accustomed to.

Vapor 1 understands that in the field of addictionology, the dynamics similar to alcohol/drug addiction can extend to other obsessive behaviors, including compulsive gambling, sex addiction, domestic violence tendencies, bullying traits, and other self-defeating behaviors.

Vapor 1 innovates and uses 98% percent of original material to treat active participants with unique substance abuse or maladaptive behavior issues. Supportive family members are encouraged to ask participants to discuss what they are learning while in this program.

Vapor 1 uses a Track Level system. Participants are required to do 22 hours of Level

II Education groups and 2 hours of individual counseling (treatment plans and reviews) for a total of 24 hours of Level II education. (Participants will randomly be given a test at the end of education sessions to assess how well they are retaining what's being presented. Participants must successfully score 70% or better to pass and go on to the next session. If they score lower than 70%, they must schedule to retake the test and pay agency costs for a retest. If the participant fails again they will be referred to a more suitable program.) Level II Therapy Tracks is based on participants' history and BAC at the time of arrest. Participants will continue to do individual sessions during Level II therapy. Level II Education and Therapy groups are 2 hours. Level II Individual counseling sessions consist of 1 hour. Participants will do an initial treatment plan and a discharge treatment plan review during Level II Education. Participants will not be allowed to move forward to Level II Therapy until the completion of their individual counseling treatment plan and treatment plan review. Participants will do an initial treatment plan and thereafter a treatment plan review after the completion of six group sessions during Level II Therapy. Participants will not be allowed to move forward to the next six sessions until the participant has completed their individual counseling treatment plan review. Treatment plan forms are located after the last chapter of the education and therapy workbooks.

Note: Get familiar with your state policies.

(Some states require treatment plan reviews every 45 days.)

Vapor 1 operates through a random BAC and UA screening system. (This is designed only for programs that are set up to do random BAC and UA screening and chooses to adopt this system.)

(Level II Education) Participants will submit 3 BACs and 1 UA during this phase per week.

(Track A) 42 therapy hours (Track B) 52 therapy hours - Participants will submit 2 BACs and 1UA during this phase per week. When Track C and D participants have completed 42 and 52 therapy hours, they will be required to submit 1 BAC and 1 UA per week.

(Track C) 68 therapy hours (Track D) 86 therapy hours - Participants will submit 1 BAC and 1UA during this phase per week.

Vapor 1 understands that to improve the participants' success rate, counselors and family members cannot afford to be permissive with participants. Permissive behavior can enable participants to stay in their addictions and behaviors.

Vapor 1 invites family members to hold participants responsible for their drinking and using behaviors.

The Vapor 1 workbook is a guide for participants to record their progress. This program is designed for participants to take an active part in their treatment process by sharing what they've learned with others and by participating in the program's exercises and worksheet activities. This program's objective is to help participants understand, although they may have experienced negative consequences because of their drinking and using behaviors. A Change of Lifestyle can occur by applying the materials this program offers to their day-to-day situations.

We have found it to be valuable for participants to complete their group sessions on time, as scheduled. It is important that participants bring their workbooks and be prepared to work during each treatment session. (Participants will not be allowed to attend groups without their workbooks.)

Feeling Journal: While in this program, participants will keep track of their feelings through journaling. Participants will stay compliant with this program by writing in their journals daily, Sunday through Saturday. Participants are encouraged to write about their strongest feelings of each day and what triggered the feeling. Participants' feeling journals will be monitored and processed at the beginning of each group (Education groups only). If the feeling journal is not up to date, the participant will not be allowed to attend the group session or be credited for that group session.

Participants will be required to complete and process their check-in/check-out worksheet after they process their feeling journal (Education groups only).

Participants will complete their weekly *Tracking Your Thinking* report and then read one affirmation from their affirmation pages that best apply to them at the time and their reasons for choosing that particular affirmation and share it with the group (Therapy groups only).

After reading and processing tracking reports and affirmations, participants will spread out for meditation and sit quietly for five minutes while listening to relaxation music (Therapy groups only).

Participants will be required to fill out a progress report and prognosis sheet at the end of each group session. This will allow participants to assess their progress through their review.

Vapor 1 is an education and therapy group course with individual counseling sessions. When participants complete an exercise or topic, a counselor of the agency the participant is enrolled in will sign, date, and write in the completed subject in their workbook. This allows the referral sources to follow along with what topics the participant has completed. At the back of their education and therapy workbook is a completion certificate. Upon completion of the program, a counselor of the agency will sign and date the certificate of completion.

In the participants' workbook, there are sign-in sheets for education group counseling sessions, therapy group counseling sessions, specialized counseling, individual counseling, community service, sign-in sheets for those in a 12-step program, and other provider contacts.

Participant workbooks have log sheets to keep note of a daily and weekly exercise schedule, log sheets to note daily and weekly participation with children's activities and involvements, log sheets to note spiritual contacts, sheets to journal feelings and thoughts, and sheets to note job searches and interviews. Participant workbooks will have log sheets to note BAC and UA testing (breath alcohol concentration and urine analysis).

Vapor 1 is aware of cultural diversity and has designed its program to allow for 12 hours of therapy in areas that apply to the participant's treatment. Examples: Talking Circle, Rope Course, Spiritual Nature Walk, Medicine Wheel, Sweat Lodge, etc. These hours will only be credited when these events are facilitated by qualified staff or specialized facilitators in the particular scope of the event. These hours will be charted on the specialized counseling sign-in sheet.

Vapor 1 has writing and drawing processing exercises toward the back part of the participant's therapy workbook. (Counselors can use these in exercises for homework assignments.)

Note: Homework assignments do not excuse participants from groups. Assignments shall be processed in the next group or viewed by the counselor. Participants will have a written test after most chapters of the education portion of workbook.

Vapor 1 invites participants, family, friends, and supporters to attend the Four Seasons Dance and Refreshments Festival as a way to celebrate the participant's sobriety in an alcohol and drug-free environment. This event will be scheduled on the second Saturday of the following months:

- March

- June

- September

- December

(Optional for programs that choose to adopt this system.)

Programs that use this system are responsible for setting up and sponsoring their events.

Vapor 1's goal is to help participants and their families come to an atonement and live life without further obligations to the legal system and disturbance in the home because of alcohol/ drug use.

Frequently Asked Questions

What determines which Track I need to do?

Your history of DUI/DWI arrests and circumstances of current arrest (blood alcohol, etc.) as mentioned earlier.

Is class participation required?
I'm shy and uncomfortable reading in front of others.

If you are uncomfortable reading in class, inform your counselor. Reading in front of the group is not mandatory. Participation is strongly encouraged during class discussions. Your class attendance and completion of assignments are required.

What if I need to miss a class?

We understand an emergency may arise which would keep you from attending a class. You are required to call and inform the counselor as soon as possible and inform him/her of your absence. An excused absence must be personally approved by your counselor.

Missed classes must be made up and unexcused absence(s) may affect your eligibility and can result in grounds for dismissal from the program.

Is there anything I can do to get through the classes sooner?

You <u>will not</u> be able to take more than one class a week. The curriculum was developed for participants to complete the program in a pre-determined time frame.

Who will best benefit from this program?

Vapor 1 is a curriculum written for participants working through a DWI/DUI.

What models does the program use?

The Vapor 1 curriculum uses Cognitive-Behavior Therapy (CBT) along with other models (mentioned earlier) to teach participants how to understand their choices and how choices can lead to unwanted consequences and perpetuate maladaptive behaviors.

What is motivational interviewing?

Motivational interviewing is a direct, participant-centered counseling style for eliciting behavior change by helping participants to explore and resolve ambivalence. Compared with non-directive counseling, it is more focused and goal-directed. The examination and resolution of ambivalence is its central purpose and the counselor is direct in pursuing this goal.

LEVEL II THERAPY REQUIREMENTS

Track	Therapy Hours	Required Time	BAC	Number of offenses
A	42	21 weeks (5 months)	.08-.199	One
B	52	26 weeks (6 months)	.20 or more	One
C	68	34 weeks (8 months)	Less than .20	Two or more
D	86	43 weeks (10 months)	.20 or more	Two or more
Level II Education Requirements	Track A 24 hours (12 weeks)	Track B 24 hours (12 weeks)	Track C 24 hours (12 weeks)	Track D 24 hours (12 weeks)

Check your state to make sure you are in compliance with all regulations.

Participants are welcome to attend Vapor Hope.

Vapor Hope
Talking Circle (Support Group)

1. Must be a current or past Vapor 1 participant or a supporter of a participant.

2. Must be on time for group. Each group starts on the hour and lasts one hour.

3. Chairs are placed in a circle.

4. Introductions

5. A maximum of two supporters are welcome.

6. Chairperson of the group signs the participant's attendance forms if needed.

7. Chairperson pulls a topic out of a bowl to share with the group. Chairperson will share about the topic while holding the Vapor sock (five minutes maximum).

8. Participants need to limit interruptions during group. (Emergencies only)

9. The Vapor sock is rotated to the left. The receiving participant will speak on the topic (three minutes maximum).

10. Participants who have nothing to say on the topic will reintroduce him/herself and state, "I am here to listen," while holding the Vapor sock and passing it on.

11. Closing thoughts: Give group members the opportunity for closing comments or questions. Group stands in a circle, holding hands, if desired, and together recites: "Hope for a better day, Hope I will laugh and play, Hope I will find my way, Hope for a better day."

12. End Meeting.

Vapor Hope is discovered to be another optional self-help support group. Vapor Hope is not coordinated by professionals in the mental health/ substance abuse field. The program is designed to allow participants to freely express daily positive and negative stressors amongst themselves.

Participants may use the hours they attended as 12 steps and self-support meetings.

Note: These hours cannot be used for counseling services.

Introduction

Way Out West

Once upon a time, there lived a hard-core hustler from the streets named Delli Dell. Over time, Delli had built himself the *salliest* (sally meaning the best, tough, bad, dope, crunk) castle in his hood. Delli was determined to keep all enemies out of his castle and live in peace. The hustler had a moat dug around his castle and filled it with alligators and piranhas. He had a draw bridge that he could lift and lower at will. Delli had guard towers on the roof equipped with gangster guards who were expert marksmen with bows and arrows. Yeah, I guess you can say Delli the hustler, was livin' large.

On one particular day, a gang of enemies rolled up on Delli's estate and they were pushin' Bentleys, Mercedes Benzs, and sally Escalades and started shooting arrows at him and his castle. Now Delli is no chump! He and his crew got right back with them and fired their arrows. However, during the shower of arrows, Delli was hit many times. When Delli's crew realized he had been hit, they rolled the hustler up and rushed him out the back door and took him to get treated for the wounds he received. As Delli lie dazed and confused on the soft comfortable couch, he began to explain to the doctor that he felt safe and protected in his castle and could hardly believe the arrows hit him. After he stopped speaking, the doctor explained to Delli that "*…the reason you were hit is because your castle was no good.*" The good doctor continued by saying, "*The arrows that hit you came from within. They were your own arrows called: fear, loneliness, rejection, inadequacy, and failure. You haven't been living in a safe haven castle; you spent a great portion of your life living in your own created prison.*"

Delli came back for a visit the next week. The doctor explained to him how hypersensitivity can lead to fears and the fear will continue to escalate if the core issue is not addressed. These fears do not go away by themselves. "*Hypersensitivity is usually a result of trauma,*" the doctor explained. The doctor discussed with Delli three common traumas that lead to hypersensitivity.

1. Neglect Trauma:
This is when healthy bonding has not taken place either as a child or an adult. This may manifest into not being able to form close relationships with others.

2. Physical Abuse Trauma:
This is when coping skills lead to physical or threatening of physical harm. This may manifest into legal and family problems.

3. Substance Abuse Trauma:

This is when the body reacts to toxins entering or exiting the nervous system that lead to maladaptive experiences. This may manifest into alcoholism or drug addiction.

The doctor ended the session by saying, *"Hypersensitivity is the hierarchy of fear."*

The next week when Delli showed up for his scheduled appointment, the doctor gave him clear examples of what self-medicating means. Self-medicating is when the following coping skills are used to disguise the fear:

Verbal -

I'm smart. I really know what I'm talking about and when that doesn't work, I start screaming, yelling, use sarcasm, or attack when things don't go my way.

Physical -

I'm in great shape and condition and when that doesn't work, I start trying to physically overpower you.

Sexual -

I'm faithful and trustworthy and when that doesn't work, I become jealous and insecure in my relationship.

Substance Abuse -

I'm clean and sober and when that doesn't work, my behaviors begin to resemble someone who is drinking and getting high.

Delli was reminded again by the doctor that his castle was no good and he continued to challenge the hustler as to why he didn't want to get better and heal. Delli attempted to use an alibi that his parents didn't give him the love and support he needed while growing up. The good doctor politely stated, *"Until you recognize and accept that your parents didn't have the capability to love and support you as children need to be, you will continue to put your ATM card in a mailbox trying to get cash back."* (Meanwhile, Delli has not accepted the things he cannot change and continues thinking that someday, the mailbox will give him money.)

The next week when Delli came to see the doctor, he said, *"Thanks for all your help,"* and shared with the good doctor that no one has ever explained things to him that way, but unfortunately Delli said, *"I cannot give up my castle. I only wanted to stop by today and tell you thanks."* Delli left and no one has seen or heard from him in over ten years. Rumor has it that Delli now lives in Kansas City and has built another castle.

A wise doctor once said, "Misery seeks company!"

Chapter 1 - 12 Steps of Growth:

PURPOSE:

To help participants manage the skills needed to reach their potential goals by recognizing familiar obstacles and addressing them.

GENERAL COMMENTS:

These steps are not your traditional AA 12 Steps that are suggested to be worked 1–12. These steps can be worked in any order that applies to the participants' needs at the time.

ACTIVITY:

Read and process feelings, thoughts, and questions.

54

A question for the provider:

Notes

Have you ever experienced a challenging growth period in your life? _______________________

What event happened? _______________________

Do you still sometimes think about it? _______________________

How do you feel now about the event? _______________________

Did you filter it with values or fears? _______________________

Values =

Responsibility

- Accept obligations
- Did the right thing in the situation/ or didn't repeat situation
- Accept accountabilities of your actions

Fears =

Avoid Responsibility

- Lack of positive thinking
- Lack of courage
- Lack of knowledge of what to do

55

12 Steps of Growth

1. Using alcohol/drugs is a way of coping with life and life's stressors, whether those stressors are positive or negative. (I like the way alcohol/drugs makes me feel.)

2. The solution requires new behaviors, new coping skills, and self-awareness. (When there's a desire, changing using habits may increase.)

3. Continuous using can lead to addiction. (My behaviors can be addictive.)

4. I can change using habits and behaviors. (When the benefits of not using overpower the consequences of using.)

5. Identifying problems and solutions in ways that work for me. (Understanding my own limitations and strengths, while setting reachable goals will help support my choices.)

6. Learn to model a new way of life. (Don't just talk the talk, demonstrate it by walking the walk.)

7. I'm willing to look at my behaviors other than my using habits. (Anger, low self-esteem, jealousy, insecurity, shame, dishonesty, hurt, fear, etc.)

8. I must stay involved and not isolate. It has been said that one of the most dangerous places on earth is too much time in my own head. (Keep in contact with supporting family and friends, coach a team, vote, and join a community activity. Do something!)

9. I believe there is more to life than the way I've been living. (There can be life without alcohol/drugs and maladaptive behaviors.)

10. I don't have to live a perfect or mistake-free life. (Just a willingness to learn from my misadventures.)

11. Come to believe my using habits and behaviors are a choice. (I will or will not do all things possible to change my habit and behaviors.)

12. I can help myself and I am responsible for my own growth. (I accept I'm not powerless over my alcohol/drug habits and behaviors.)

Chapter 2 - 12 Community Tragedies

PURPOSE:

To help participants identify values and reconstruct what is most important in life.

GENERAL COMMENTS:

Discuss each tragedy with participants and advise them throughout this course that they may randomly be asked what community tragedy they can identify with at this time in their life. Once they identify a tragedy they may be asked, which of the 12 steps of growth are they working on that will help them better deal with the tragedy.

ACTIVITY:

Read and process feelings, thoughts, and questions.

58

A question for the provider:

Notes

Have you ever experienced a personal tragedy in your life?

What event happened?

Do you still sometimes think about it?

How do you feel now about the event?

Did you filter it with values or fears?

Values =

Responsibility

- Accept obligations
- Did the right thing in the situation/ or didn't repeat situation
- Accept accountabilities of your actions

Fears =

Avoid Responsibility

- Lack of positive thinking
- Lack of courage
- Lack of knowledge of what to do

59

Lendell L Jones

12 Community Tragedies:

Self-Inflicted Sufferings

1. **Carjacking-** inability to obtain or maintain own transportation

2. **Victim-** succumbing to the pressures of others

3. **Addiction-** maladaptive behavior continues regardless of consequences

4. **Gambling-** putting oneself in high-risk situations, thereby setting oneself up for failure

5. **Pimping-** the exploitation of an individual or system for self-benefit

6. **Hoeing-** the exploitation of self for personal gain

7. **Hustling-** deception of others for personal benefit

8. **Gangbanging-** surrendering self to the will of others in order to be part of the group

9. **Unsafe Sex-** living a promiscuous lifestyle

10. **Poverty-** living a poor lifestyle regardless of financial standing

11. **Welfare-** neglecting responsibilities and relying on others for support

12. **Unemployment-** loss of opportunity to support oneself

Chapter 3 - 12 Choices in Life

PURPOSE:

To introduce the concept of choice to participants as a tool and guiding point in their lives.

GENERAL COMMENTS:

Discuss with participants the power they have by making their own choices in life.

ACTIVITY:

Read and process feelings, thoughts, and questions. Discuss with participants the power they have in making their own choices in life.

62

Lendell L Jones

O.C. Original Counselor

A question for the provider:

Notes

Have you ever had to make a tough choice in your life?

____

What event happened? _______________________________

Do you still sometimes think about it? _______________________________

How do you feel now about the event? _______________________________

Did you filter it with values or fears? _______________________________

Values =

Responsibility

- Accept obligations
- Did the right thing in the situation/ or didn't repeat situation
- Accept accountabilities of your actions

Fears =

Avoid Responsibility

- Lack of positive thinking
- Lack of courage
- Lack of knowledge of what to do

63

12 Choices in Life:

1. I have the choice to be alcohol and drug-free.

2. I have the choice to be in healthy relationships.

3. I have the choice to be responsible.

4. I have the choice to respect myself and others.

5. I have the choice to set healthy boundaries.

6. I have the choice to be educated.

7. I have the choice to make good decisions.

8. I have the choice to change my situations.

9. I have the choice to work for success.

10. I have the choice to try.

11. I have the choice to be free.

12. I have the choice to believe.

Chapter 4 - Delli Dell's Story:

PURPOSE:

Follow the dynamics of Delli Dell as he comes to terms with how his choices are affecting his behaviors and outcome.

GENERAL COMMENTS:

Optional strategies for facilitators:

1. Have participants read the story individually and then process with the group.

2. Have participants go around the group table or circle and each participant read one paragraph and then process with the group.

3. Have participants separate into groups and have a pre-selected person read the story to the individual group. The individual groups discuss the story before coming back to the group as a whole, then process.

4. Facilitator reads the story to the group and then allows the group to process.

ACTIVITY:

Facilitator will have participants read Delli Dell's Story and process the events of his story.

66

Notes

Have you ever experienced someone telling you that you're too smart for your own good in your life? ____________________

What event happened? ____________________
____
____

Do you still sometimes think about it? ____________________
____
____

How do you feel now about the event? ____________________
____
____

Did you filter it with values or fears? ____________________
____
____

Values =

Responsibility

- Accept obligations
- Did the right thing in the situation/ or didn't repeat situation
- Accept accountabilities of your actions

Fears =

Avoid Responsibility

- Lack of positive thinking
- Lack of courage
- Lack of knowledge of what to do

67

Lendell L Jones

Delli Dell's Story

Denial: "Why Me?"

I bet if I was anyone else, I wouldn't have to come to these domestic violence classes. I mean, all I did was push my wife down and smack her a few times. Come on, who doesn't do that every now and again? I think the judge has had a vendetta against me ever since he sentenced me to probation nine months ago, after receiving my second DWI. What I don't understand: why is everybody concerned about what I do? If I choose to drink and drive, that is my business and my business alone. It's not as if I get so drunk that I can't handle it or don't know what I'm doing. My core belief is, this is my body and it shouldn't matter to anyone else what I do with it. Besides, I like the way alcohol makes me feel.

Yeah, I see the news reports and I read all the scare tactics about impaired drivers, but you know what, I have not been in a drinking and driving accident one time in my life and I've been doing this for years. So I can't see how anyone would think I'm a threat to society when I have a few drinks in me and take to the wheel. The truth of the matter, I think I'm an expert at drinking and driving. Ya know! If you really think about it, the judge should have sentenced me to teach a class on how to drink and drive safely. Like I said, I've been drinking and driving for years and haven't been in one drinking and driving accident.

To make matters more stressful for me, my wife and the children continue nagging me about my drug use. What's up with that? I go to work five days a week. I pay my bills on time, most of the time. So what if I like to hang out and kick it with my friends sometimes? I deserve to get high because life is tough and getting high helps take the edge off. Another thing, I would like to know where it is written that I have to attend all of my son's football games. Can't I get my propers? I attended two of them and as far as I am concerned, that's two more than I had to. I still can't believe my daughter is upset with me. I admit I promised her I would attend the father/student field trip with her, but can't she understand people have the right to change their minds? Besides, if I would have shown up for her field trip I probably would have embarrassed her because frankly, I was extremely high that day. My wife? I have no idea what planet she is from. Can you believe it? She is claiming that my usage is interfering with our relationship. I don't know where she came up with that conclusion. I offered her to get high with me. Maybe if she accepted my invitation we could take the rough edges of life off together. However, being the stubborn, self-righteous person she is, her answer is always, "Absolutely not!"

Did you know when I drink and get high I seem to feel better about myself? I guess it could be said that alcohol and drugs are esteem boosters. You should see me. I'm the life of any party when I'm under the influence. As a matter of fact, I sometimes believe I'm ten feet tall and bulletproof when I'm drinking and getting high. Now! Are you beginning to see why I enjoy the party life? This lifestyle does so much for me. I sincerely think it is ridiculous for the judge, my family, or anyone else to even suggest I change my lifestyle. Can't you see the way I'm living is large and who in their right state of mind wouldn't want to live like this! So my message to the judge: "You may think you have the upper hand, but when I complete this program I'll be right back to my old bag of tricks. Ya dig?"

Chapter 5 - Locus of Control

PURPOSE:

Give participants a better understanding of internal and external messages which are then processed.

GENERAL COMMENTS:

Draw two circles on the board and explain and discuss the internal and external theory of Locus of Control with participants and be prepared to answer questions and statements.

ACTIVITY:

Fill in the missing words.

70

A question for the provider:

Notes

Have you ever been caught between external and internal control in your life? ___________________________

What event happened? ___________________________
____
____

Do you still sometimes think about it? ______________
____
____

How do you feel now about the event? ______________
____
____

Did you filter it with values or fears? ______________
____
____

Values =

Responsibility

- Accept obligations
- Did the right thing in the situation/ or didn't repeat situation
- Accept accountabilities of your actions

Fears =

Avoid Responsibility

- Lack of positive thinking
- Lack of courage
- Lack of knowledge of what to do

71

Lendell L Jones

Locus of Control

Locus of Control is a person's belief about what causes positive or negative outcomes in life. This belief can apply to every area of one's existence. Individuals with high internal locus of control believe outcomes are designed from their own actions and behaviors. This type places much of their success and failures within. Individuals with high external locus of control believe outcomes are designed from the power of others. This type places much of their success and failures on others.

The pattern usually goes as follows:

External: *Received messages*

Relationships

- My partner makes me happy

- If my partner quit a certain behavior, we'd be fine

- My partner knows what's best for me

- My partner will make it right

- If only my partner would make things right

Employment

- My boss won't give me a break

- This job is who I am

- This job has me trapped

- This job is destroying my family

- This company will give me a break, someday

The Law

- If there weren't so many police, I wouldn't get DWIs

- The man keeps holding me down

- Removing the drug dealers will cure my addiction

- I can't change the law

- The law will hold me accountable

Society

- The world is prejudiced against me

- They'll never let my kind become president

- They'll always give us the cheap jobs

- My teachers will fail me

- The world says I'm a loser

> *Locus of Control originates from one's:*
>
> - *Thinking*
>
> - *Feelings*
>
> - *Perceptions*
>
> *Which then leads to **behaviors** that ultimately determine the **outcome** (consequence). Either the outcome will be good or bad.*

Internal: *Broadcast messages*

Relationships

- My partner and I are happy together

- My partner and I both have flaws

- I am responsible for my actions

- I accept challenges

- My partner can't fix me

Employment

- I have to create my own breaks

- This job is what I do, not who I am

- This job is another opportunity

- I am allowing my work to affect my family

- I have the skills to move ahead

The Law

- If I quit drinking and driving, I won't get DWIs

- I keep holding myself down (self-defeating behaviors)

- The dealers are not my problem, I am

- I can vote and change my behaviors and attitude

- I hold myself accountable to the law

Society

- I recognize my prejudices and judgments

- I can run for presidency if I choose to

- I can work hard and achieve any position I choose

- I won't allow anyone to fail me

- I'm a winner in many areas of my life

Chapter 6 - Domestic Violence

PURPOSE:

To identify some of the beliefs and behavioral patterns that can have long-lasting effects on families and communities.

GENERAL COMMENTS:

Learn to let go of old ways of thinking and behaving and begin to set healthy boundaries. Invite participants to do their own research for more updated information.

ACTIVITY:

1. Discuss Domestic Violence as a group or with individual participants.

2. Ask participants if they have anything to add.

3. Allow participants to share their direct or indirect experiences with Domestic Violence.

A question for the provider:

Notes

Have you ever been faced with domestic violence in your life?

____

What event happened? _______________________________

____

____

Do you still sometimes think about it? _______________

____

____

How do you feel now about the event? _______________

____

____

Did you filter it with values or fears? _______________

____

____

Values =

Responsibility

- Accept obligations
- Did the right thing in the situation/ or didn't repeat situation
- Accept accountabilities of your actions

Fears =

Avoid Responsibility

- Lack of positive thinking
- Lack of courage
- Lack of knowledge of what to do

Lendell L Jones

Domestic Violence

Domestic violence is a type of behavior. It involves injuring another person, usually a spouse or partner. However, it can also be a child, parent, or sibling.

Domestic violence is a serious problem. It is a common cause of injury. Victims may suffer physical injuries such as bruises or broken bones. They may suffer emotionally from depression, anxiety, or social isolation.

It is hard to know exactly how common domestic violence is because people often don't report it. There is no typical victim. Domestic violence is also known as domestic abuse, spousal abuse, or intimate partner violence. Domestic violence occurs when a family member, partner, or ex-partner attempts to physically or psychologically dominate another. Domestic violence often refers to violence between spouses though the truth is, domestic violence often happens within non-married or intimate partners. Domestic violence occurs in all cultures: people of all races, ethnicities, religions, sexes, and classes can be perpetrators of domestic violence. It affects those of all levels of income and education. Domestic violence is perpetrated by both men and women.

Domestic violence traits:

- Assault (reasonable threat to person)

- Battery (requires actual contact to a person)

- Stalking

- Kidnapping

- False imprisonment

- Any criminal offense resulting in physical injury or death

Perpetrators often try to dominate and control other people. They use intimidation, shame, guilt, anger, and fear to wear down and gain complete power over the victim. Perpetrators may threaten the victim, hurt the victim, or hurt those around the victim (children, family, victim support team) and sometimes even threaten to hurt and actually hurt themselves.

These traits are used for one purpose: to gain and maintain total control over the victim. In addition, perpetrators use the following tactics to exert power over the victim:

Pattern of Domestic Violence

Abuse -

The perpetrator uses violent behaviors as a communication tool: "You do as I say or I will hurt you."

Guilt -

The perpetrator often feels guilt after a violent episode. This does not mean the violence won't occur again. The perpetrator does have a "calm period" and may treat the victim kindly during this time. (Classic case of flowers, candy, and violence.)

Blame, Minimize, Justify, and Excuses -

Denial becomes the perpetrator's best friend. As long as the perpetrator has someone or something to blame these behaviors on, they can minimize the extremity of the behavior, passing off responsibility: other people have done worst (justify). They may have a hundred and one excuses as to why they do what they do, to justify their behaviors: "If you only knew how bad my day was, you wouldn't make me angry."

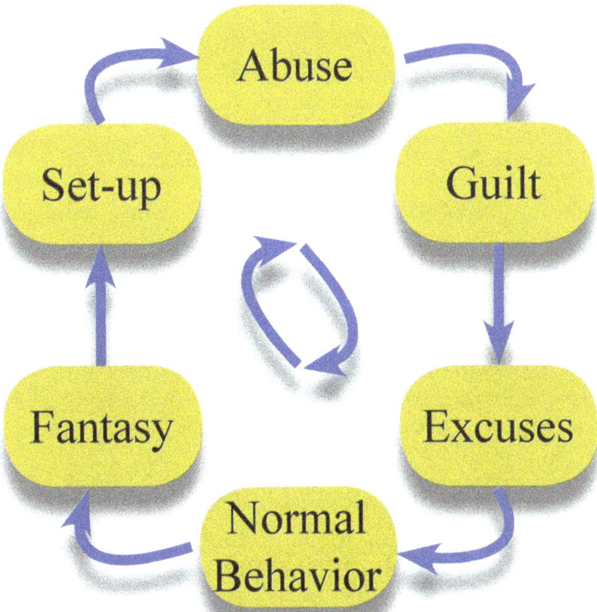

"Normal" Behavior -

Much of the time the perpetrator is a masterful charmer and will do anything to keep the victim in the relationship. They may revert back to the beginning of the relationship when things were good and start living in that scene again. Perpetrators often become well attentive to the victim and shower them with welcomed attention. Perpetrators do not want to lose their victims.

Fantasy and Planning -

The perpetrator often fantasizes about abusing their victim. They may be triggered by anything that will get them to start thinking about how the victim wronged them. Once the fantasy has become clear, the perpetrator can then start planning ways to get back at their victim.

Set-up -

The perpetrator can then set the victim up by creating situations to justify the violence or behaviors (entrapment).

Violent Statistics

A recent 32-nation study by the University of New Hampshire found that female students initiate partner violence as often as male students and that controlling behavior exists equally in perpetrators of both sexes.

According to the Stalking Resource Center:

- 1,006,970 women and 370,990 men are stalked annually in the United States.

- 1 in 12 women and 1 in 45 men will be stalked in their lifetime.

- 77% of female and 64% of male victims know their stalker.

- 87% of stalkers are men.

- 59% of female victims and 30% of male victims are stalked by an intimate partner.

- 81% of women stalked by a current or former intimate partner are also physically abused by that partner.

- 31% of women stalked by a current or former intimate partner are also sexually abused by that partner.

- The average duration of stalking is 1.8 years.

- If the stalking involves an intimate partner, the average duration of stalking increases to 2.2 years.

- 61% of stalkers made unwanted phone calls, 33% sent or left unwanted letters or items, 29% vandalized property, and 9% killed or threatened to kill a family pet.

- 28% of female victims and 10% of male victims obtained a protective order. 69% of female victims and 81% of male victims had the protection order violated.

- 76% of femicide victims had been stalked by the person who killed them.

- 67% had been physically abused by their intimate partner.

- 89% of femicide victims who had been physically abused had also been stalked in the 12 months before the murder.

- 79% of abused femicide victims reported stalking during the same period that they reported abuse.

- 85% of attempted femicide cases involve at least one episode of stalking within 12 months prior to the attempted femicide.

- 54% of femicide victims reported stalking to police before they were killed by their stalkers.

If you are being abused, you need to have a plan in place so that you can leave: when to go, where to go, and how to stay away.

Call the <u>National Domestic Violence Hotline</u> at 1-800-799-7233 (SAFE) for advice and help with your escape.

If you need help immediately, call **911**.

Chapter 7 - Impaired Drivers (Laws and Beyond)

PURPOSE:

To combat the high risk of drinking and driving while becoming knowledgeable about the penalties.

GENERAL COMMENTS:

Every day an average of 13 people between the ages of 16 and 24 die in an alcohol-related crash. Invite participants to do their own research for more updated information.

ACTIVITY:

Read and process feelings, thoughts, and questions.

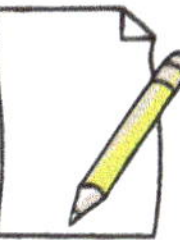

Notes

Have you ever been in a situation in your life where you had to choose between drinking and driving? _________________

What event happened? _____________________________
____
____

Do you still sometimes think about it? _______________
____
____

How do you feel now about the event? _______________
____
____

Did you filter it with values or fears? _______________
____
____

Values =

Responsibility

- Accept obligations
- Did the right thing in the situation/ or didn't repeat situation
- Accept accountabilities of your actions

Fears =

Avoid Responsibility

- Lack of positive thinking
- Lack of courage
- Lack of knowledge of what to do

81

Impaired Drivers - Laws and Beyond

To be considered an impaired driver while operating a vehicle, the driver must have a BAC of .01 or greater or be under the influence of a psychoactive substance.

BAC is the blood alcohol concentration in the body.

Various states may have different BAC levels to determine if a driver is over the legal limit to operate a vehicle. .08 is the national standard. For drivers under the age of 21, most states have a zero tolerance. .02 could qualify underage drivers for a DWI.

Most DWI convictions are categorized as misdemeanors. When alcohol or other drugs caused bodily injury this can be classified as a felony. Some states consider multiple DWIs a felony even though no bodily injury or death was related during the time of arrest.

What does Per Se mean?

Per Se or Driving With Excessive Content is driving with an alcohol level equal to or greater than .08 and does not require erratic driving.

What does Presumption mean?

Being observed driving erratically or dangerously due to alcohol or drug use.

The national BAC standard is .08 or greater. Both Per Se and Presumption can lead to DWI arrest and conviction.

When a driver is charged with DWI, there are four possible outcomes:

1. A plea of No Contest - usually this applies to first-time offenders.

2. A deferred judgment or sentences - usually this is applied to first-time offenders.

3. Found not guilty

4. A conviction

Convicted DWI offenders in most states are reported on their court records and the Department of Motor Vehicle (DMV). The DMV may take action against a driver charged with DWI under the Administrative License Revocation Law.

Driving while ability is impaired (DWAI) is used in some states. Also, skiing, skateboarding, boating, roller-blading, and flying can be considered OWI (operating while impaired).

DWI penalties vary from state to state. Common court actions for DWI offenders:

- Incarceration

- Fines, restitution, or community service

- Alcohol/drug evaluation to measure the need for treatment

- Probation

- Specialized drunk drivers programs

- In or outpatient treatment

- Random urine and breath screening

- Ignition interlocks

- 12 steps or self-help meetings

- Electronic monitoring

Department of Motor Vehicle common actions for DWI offenders:

Suspension of driving license (the length of time varies from state to state). Much of the time it is determined by the number of prior DWI offenses and the level of BAC at the time of arrest.

Some states have a lifetime driving suspension with no chance of hardship for repeated DWI offenders.

Probationary licenses are offered by some states with restrictions to a driver who lost his/her license due to a DWI offense. Often this is designed for first-time offenders.

Reinstatement requirements vary from state to state. Generally, the requirements are a successful completion of an alcohol/drug treatment program, proof of insurance, and payment of a reinstatement fee.

Revocation is designed for repeat DWI offenders and is usually set for a minimum of one year or longer.

Administrative License Revocation is designed to allow an officer to inspect a suspected impaired driver to submit a BAC or urine test immediately to remove the driver from the road.

For a driver that refuses to submit the required test or have a BAC of .08 or greater, the result is usually revocation. Driving privileges are generally suspended for a few months up to a year. Revocation often depends on the driver's BAC level.

Ignition interlocks are required by many states before licenses can be reinstated.

Interstate Driver's License Compacts

Most states will accept DWI treatment and education when requirements are met from another state.

The offender must provide proof of completing DUI treatment and education requirements in the new area of residence to the MVD before reinstatement will be approved.

The Danger

When a driver operates a vehicle while impaired, the offenders put themselves and others in physical danger.

There are about 1.5 million DWI citations a year. One-third of these citations are repeat offenders.

- About 25,000 alcohol-related traffic fatalities occur each year in the United States.

- Over 100,000 deaths occur each year due to the effects of alcohol.

- 5% of all deaths from diseases of the circulatory system are attributed to alcohol.

- 15% of all deaths from diseases of the respiratory system are attributed to alcohol.

- 30% of all deaths from accidents caused by fire and flames are attributed to alcohol.

- 30% of all accidental drownings are attributed to alcohol.

- 30% of all suicides are attributed to alcohol.

- 40% of all deaths due to accidental falls are attributed to alcohol.

- 45% of all deaths in automobile accidents are attributed to alcohol.

- 60% of all homicides are attributed to alcohol.

Chapter 8 - The Body, Alcohol, and Society

PURPOSE:

To recognize the consequence of making poor choices or taking unnecessary risks.

GENERAL COMMENTS:

For every decision you make, there can be consequences.

ACTIVITY:

Read and process feelings, thoughts, and questions.

Lendell L Jones

O.C. Original Counselor

Notes

Have you ever experienced being drunk as a skunk or high as a kite in your life? _______________________

What event happened? _______________________

Do you still sometimes think about it? _______________________

How do you feel now about the event? _______________________

Did you filter it with values or fears? _______________________

Values =

Responsibility

- Accept obligations
- Did the right thing in the situation/ or didn't repeat situation
- Accept accountabilities of your actions

Fears =

Avoid Responsibility

- Lack of positive thinking
- Lack of courage
- Lack of knowledge of what to do

87

The Body, Alcohol, and Society

The more body fat a person has, the longer it takes for the alcohol to metabolize and leave the body.

> *A 12 oz. can of beer, 5 oz. of wine, or 1.5 oz. of hard liquor all takes about one hour to leave the average human body.*

Drinking alcohol heavily increases the risk of developing:

- High blood pressure

- Pancreatitis (severe inflammation of the pancreas)

- Damage to unborn babies in pregnant women

- Cancers (mouth, gullet, liver, colon, and breast)

- Damage to nervous tissue

- Serious liver problems (alcoholic liver disease)

- Sexual difficulties such as impotence

- Stomach disorders

- Obesity (alcohol has a high-calorie content)

- Muscle and heart disease

- Alcohol dependence (addiction)

- Mental health problems including depression and anxiety

Drinking too much alcohol can lead to three types of liver conditions:

Fatty liver -
A build-up of fat occurs within liver cells, common in people who drink heavily, and regularly. Fatty liver is not usually serious and causes symptoms and usually is reversible if you stop drinking heavily. However, with continuous heavy drinking, it can progress and the body develops hepatitis.

Alcohol hepatitis -

Inflammation of the liver. This can lead to jaundice, blood clotting problems, confusion, bleeding into the gut, coma, and eventually cause cirrhosis, and is oftentimes fatal.

Alcoholic cirrhosis -

Cirrhosis is a condition where normal liver tissue is replaced by scar tissue (fibrosis). Liver cells become damaged and die as scar tissue gradually develops. As this happens, the liver gradually loses its ability to function well. Cirrhosis of the liver is often fatal.

Social Problems and Alcohol:

Alcohol can affect social living in many ways:

Family problems -

Arguments, domestic violence, neglect of responsibilities, infidelity, and numerous marriage breakups have been attributed to alcohol.

Work -

Alcohol can lead to unemployment, calling in sick to work, not doing the job to the fullest capability and work-related accidents.

Personal relationships -

Sometimes people who drink heavily get involved with negative people and eventually hurt the ones who care most about them. This can also lead to illegal activities such as drinking and driving and other crimes.

Throughout this course, participants may realize that many areas in their life may need a change of lifestyle. However, we invite each participant to stay focused on the changes that they can and will do in the present moment.

On Your Mark, Get Set, Let's Go To Work!

Chapter 9 - Driver's Impairment

PURPOSE:

To improve awareness of how fatal drinking and driving can be.

GENERAL COMMENTS:

People under 25 have the highest violation rate in all 6 of the following categories. Invite participants to research current statistics.

1. Not yielding right-of-way
2. Improper passing
3. Speeding
4. Illegal turning
5. Driving under the influence of alcohol/drugs
6. Ignoring traffic control devices

ACTIVITY:

Read and process feelings, thoughts, and questions.

90

Notes

Have you ever experienced being charged with a DWI/DUI in your life? ______________

What event happened? ______________

Do you still sometimes think about it? ______________

How do you feel now about the event? ______________

Did you filter it with values or fears? ______________

Values =

Responsibility

- Accept obligations
- Did the right thing in the situation/ or didn't repeat situation
- Accept accountabilities of your actions

Fears =

Avoid Responsibility

- Lack of positive thinking
- Lack of courage
- Lack of knowledge of what to do

91

Driver's Impairment

The 50 states in the U.S. including Puerto Rico apply two statutory offenses to drivers under the influence of alcohol. The first offense is driving under the influence (DUI). The second, driving while intoxicated/impaired (DWI), or operating a motor vehicle while intoxicated/impaired. This is based upon the arresting officer's observations. (Drivers are given a road sobriety test, the arresting officer screens the driver's behaviors, speech, mood affect, etc.)

"Illegal per se" is known as the second offense, which is operating a vehicle with a BAC of 0.08% or higher. It is illegal in all 50 states including Puerto Rico to drive with a BAC that is 0.08% or above.

In 2007, there were 14,465 fatalities in crashes involving drivers with a BAC of .08 and above, 34% of the total traffic fatalities for the year. This represents an average of one alcohol-related driving fatality every 32 minutes.

Drivers involved in alcohol-related fatal crashes are four times higher at night than during the day.

The percentage of drivers with BAC of .08 or above in fatal crashes is highest for motorcycle operators (27%), followed by light trucks (24%), and then passenger cars (23%). The percentage of drivers with BAC levels of .08 or higher in fatal crashes has been reordered the lowest for large trucks (1%).

The percentage of drivers in a fatal crash with a BAC level of .08 or above was for drivers ages 21–24 (33%), followed by ages 25–34 (29%), and 35–44 (25%).

Drivers with a BAC of .08 or above involved in fatal crashes were eight times more likely to have had a prior conviction for drunk driving with a BAC of .08 or above.

Drivers involved in fatal crashes who had been drinking with a BAC of .08 or above, male drivers comprise about 81% of all drivers.

Alcohol-related deaths in the United States since 1982:

Year	Total fatalities	Alcohol-related fatalities	
		Number	Percent
1982	43,945	26,173	60
1983	42,589	24,635	58
1984	44,257	24,762	56
1985	43,825	23,167	53
1986	46,087	25,017	54
1987	46,390	24,094	52
1988	47,087	23,833	51
1989	45,582	22,424	49
1990	44,599	22,587	51
1991	41,508	20,159	49
1992	39,250	18,290	47
1993	40,150	17,908	45
1994	40,716	17,308	43
1995	41,817	17,732	42
1996	42,065	17,749	42
1997	42,013	16,711	40
1998	41,501	16,673	40
1999	41,717	16,572	40
2000	41,945	17,380	41
2001	42,196	17,400	41
2002	43,005	17,524	41
2003	42,643	17,013	40
2004	42,518	16,919	39
2005	43,443	16,885	39
2006	42,532	15,829	37
2007	41,059	15,387	37

Drinking and driving fatalities by state in 2007 (ranked by highest number of alcohol-related deaths):

State	Total Fatalities	Alcohol-Related Fatalities	
		Number	Percent
Texas	3,466	**1,544**	45%
California	4,229	1,509	36%
Florida	3,363	1,111	33%
Pennsylvania	1,517	556	37%
Illinois	1,254	540	43%
Georgia	1,688	539	32%
Arizona	1,280	502	39%
North Carolina	1,558	490	31%
New York	1,454	483	33%
Tennessee	1,286	478	37%
South Carolina	1,037	477	46%
Missouri	1,087	469	43%
Ohio	1,235	451	37%
Alabama	1,206	445	37%
Louisiana	982	425	43%
Michigan	1,081	390	36%
Mississippi	911	358	39%
Wisconsin	722	352	49%
Virginia	961	347	36%
Indiana	896	290	32%
New Jersey	771	285	37%
Washington	630	269	43%
Kentucky	913	257	28%
Arkansas	665	245	37%
Oklahoma	765	243	32%
Maryland	651	235	36%
Colorado	533	207	39%
Oregon	477	177	37%

Lendell L Jones

O.C. Original Counselor

Minnesota	493	175	36%
Nevada	432	168	39%
Kansas	466	162	35%
Massachusetts	422	159	38%
New Mexico	484	155	32%
West Virginia	408	155	38%
Iowa	439	142	32%
Connecticut	301	121	40%
Montana	255	114	45%
Idaho	267	102	38%
Nebraska	266	86	32%
South Dakota	191	78	41%
Wyoming	195	78	40%
Hawaii	160	77	48%
Maine	188	70	37%
Utah	284	63	22%
New Hampshire	127	51	40%
Delaware	148	50	34%
North Dakota	111	47	42%
Rhode Island	81	37	46%
Vermont	86	28	33%
Alaska	73	23	31%
Dist of Columbia	37	14	36%
National	**42,532**	**15,829**	**37%**
Puerto Rico	507	176	35%

*According to the National Highway Traffic Safety Administration (NHTSA), "A motor vehicle crash is considered to be alcohol-related if at least one driver or non-occupant (such as a pedestrian or bicyclist) involved in the crash is determined to have had a blood alcohol concentration (BAC) of .01 gram per deciliter (g/dL) or higher. Thus, any fatality that occurs in an alcohol-related crash is considered an alcohol-related fatality. The term 'alcohol-related' does not indicate that a crash or fatality was caused by the presence of alcohol."

Chapter 10 - Guest Speaker

PURPOSE:

To give participants a view of what life can be like when not using.

GENERAL COMMENTS:

Recovering addict will share their story from the fall to the come-up.

ACTIVITY:

Ask questions and gather information about support group communities and resources.

Lendell L Jones   O.C. Original Counselor

A question for the provider:

Notes

Have you ever been in a situation in your life where you had to choose to either lie or tell the truth, and the truth could bring you negative consequences? _______________________

What event happened? _______________________
____
____

Do you still sometimes think about it? _______________________
____
____

How do you feel now about the event? _______________________
____
____

Did you filter it with values or fears? _______________________
____
____

Values =

Responsibility

- Accept obligations
- Did the right thing in the situation/ or didn't repeat situation
- Accept accountabilities of your actions

Fears =

Avoid Responsibility

- Lack of positive thinking
- Lack of courage
- Lack of knowledge of what to do

97

Chapter 11 - Recovering from Addiction

Drugs and the Consequences

PURPOSE:

To explore the drug families and their effects.

GENERAL COMMENTS:

Many legal drugs have been proven to provide physical and emotional benefits. Inform participants that this program was written many years ago and invite them to research modern-day statistics.

ACTIVITY:

Read and process feelings, thoughts, and questions.

98

A question for the provider:

Notes

Have you ever used illicit drugs that led to consequences in your life? _______________________________

What event happened? _______________________________
____
____

Do you still sometimes think about it? _______________________________
____
____

How do you feel now about the event? _______________________________
____
____

Did you filter it with values or fears? _______________________________
____
____

Values =
Responsibility

- Accept obligations
- Did the right thing in the situation/ or didn't repeat situation
- Accept accountabilities of your actions

Fears =
Avoid Responsibility

- Lack of positive thinking
- Lack of courage
- Lack of knowledge of what to do

99

Lendell L Jones

Drugs and the Consequences

Alcohol Family
Beer, Spirits, Wine

Impaired judgment can lead to bad decisions, alcohol dependence, health, family, and legal issues.

Opiates Family
Codeine, Heroin, Morphine

Impaired psychological and social functioning can lead to physical withdrawal, depression, impaired memory, insomnia, sleepiness, and coma.

Depressants Family -
Barbiturates, Tranquilizers, Methaqualone

Impaired judgment can lead to dependency, tolerance, withdrawals, slow heartbeat, seizures, stupor, staggering, agitation, insomnia, and coma.

Stimulants Family
Ecstasy, Cocaine, Amphetamines, Methamphetamines

Impaired judgment can lead to dependency, tolerance, rapid heartbeat, hallucinations, delusional thinking, paranoia, depression, weight loss, suicidal thoughts, and agitation.

Inhalants Family
Paint, Nitrous Oxide, Gasoline, Amyl Nitrate

Impaired memory or attention can lead to dependency, painful withdrawals, muscle aches, fever, diarrhea, malnutrition, slurred speech, hepatitis, reduced sex drive, thirst, hunger, fatigue, drowsiness, and coma.

Cannabis Family
Hash, Marijuana

Impaired judgment can lead to psychological dependence, tolerance, impairment of short-term memory, mental confusion, increased heart rate, impaired reproductive ability, decreased motivation, distorted reality, hallucinations, paranoia, and distrust; increases the risk of lung cancer and decreases normal interests.

Hallucinogens Family

Peyote, LSD, Mushrooms, Phencyclidine (PCP)

Impaired judgment can lead to flashbacks after usage stops, intolerance, suspicion, distrust, paranoia, distorted reality, violence, hallucinations, delusional thinking, rapid heartbeat, convulsions, and coma.

All the drugs listed above except for alcohol are listed as scheduled drugs under the Controlled Substance Act of the United States. Required for drugs to be placed as scheduled, are the following:

1. The drug or other substance has a high potential for abuse.

2. Excluding marijuana, drugs and other substances currently have no medical use in treatment in the United States.

3. There is a lack of accepted safety for use of the drug or other substance under medical supervision.

2007 - Causes of Drug-Related Death in the United States:	
Tobacco	435.001
Alcohol	85.209
Adverse reaction to prescription drugs	32,198
All illicit drug use, direct and indirect	17,027

Before coming into treatment/counseling how often did you use?
(Do not include tobacco.)

____

[ ] One to two times per month.

[ ] One to two times per week.

[ ] Two to three times per week.

[ ] Four to five times per week

[ ] Six to seven times per week

How often do you use tobacco?

____

[ ] None

[ ] One to five cigarettes per day.

[ ] Six to ten cigarettes per day.

[ ] Ten to fifteen cigarettes per day.

[ ] Fifteen to a pack per day.

[ ] More.

Chapter 12 - Building Self-Esteem

PURPOSE:

Gain insight on how self-esteem and value systems correlate.

GENERAL COMMENTS:

I think, I perceive, I feel, I behave.

ACTIVITY:

Discussion and fill in the blanks.

102

A question for the provider:

Have you ever had low self-esteem in your life? _________

What event happened? ______________________________
____
____

Do you still sometimes think about it? _______________
____
____

How do you feel now about the event? _______________
____
____

Did you filter it with values or fears? _______________
____
____

Values =

Responsibility

- Accept obligations
- Did the right thing in the situation/ or didn't repeat situation
- Accept accountabilities of your actions

Fears =

Avoid Responsibility

- Lack of positive thinking
- Lack of courage
- Lack of knowledge of what to do

103

Building Self-Esteem

What is self-esteem? Self-esteem is a judgment of how you perceive yourself.

What is self-confidence? Self-confidence is the ability to believe in yourself and to achieve or accomplish a goal or task.

Is it possible to have low self-esteem about self, yet be self-confident?

Absolutely!

> **Example:** *Farmer John was very confident in getting his crops to produce. However, Farmer John felt worthless as a husband and father. This no doubt increased his feeling of inadequacy.*

Often self-esteem dictates our behaviors and therefore, our outcome.

> **Example:** *Billy Gates thought he was a prepared, senior quarterback for his high school football team. He felt well prepared, he perceived himself as being prepared, he played on that cool, homecoming night as a well-prepared player and by the end of the game, he was pleased with his performance.*

> **Example:** *Tommy Six thought he wasn't smart enough to keep up with his advanced chemistry class in college. He felt like an outcast. He perceived himself as being a dummy. He then began to neglect his class time and study time, which obviously he wasn't prepared for. By the end of the semester, he wasn't pleased with his grade and failed the course. Low self-esteem leads to self-defeating behaviors, and those self-defeating behaviors lead to negative outcomes.*

How does alcohol abuse or chemical dependency affect your self-esteem? It doesn't, although often people use alcohol and drugs with the false hopes that these substances will make them feel better. Sometimes these products, along with impulsive, addictive, and other self-defeating behaviors can be temporarily perceived as productive. Remember, self-esteem is how you feel about yourself. So it doesn't matter what you do to alter your senses and feelings because ultimately people, places, and things fade or wear off, and once again, you are stuck with yourself. That's why you will not find a single person who has a positive self-esteem abusing alcohol, drugs, or another human being. Think about it. If you felt good about yourself, why would you want to change how you feel by adding a mood-altering substance to your body and mind? Or why would you have the need to downplay another person instead of building that person up?

Another example may help you understand more about self-esteem: It would sound a little silly to go to the dope dealer or bootlegger at two or three o'clock in the morning and say, "Dope, man. Give me some of that stuff that makes me feel how I feel because I feel wonderful about myself." That sounds silly because why would anyone with high self-esteem put themselves or family in harm's way by turning to alcohol, drugs, unhealthy relationships, or other impulsive or self-defeating behaviors?

Self-Esteem

Unveiling a better you

What are five things you could do that would increase your self-esteem? ___________________
____
____
____
____

How old were you when you felt the worst and your self-esteem was the lowest? _____________

What were the situations or events that led to those feelings? ___________________________
____
____
____

If you had better self-esteem, how would your life improve? ____________________________
____
____
____

What is your biggest fear of others finding out you have low self-esteem?_________________
____
____
____

Who in your family would you say has the highest self-esteem?__________________________

Why do you think this family member has high self-esteem? ____________________________
____
____

Chapter 13 - How to Build Self-Esteem

PURPOSE:

Gain insight on how self-esteem and value systems correlate.

GENERAL COMMENTS:

I think, I perceive, I feel, I behave.

ACTIVITY:

Discussion and fill in the blanks.

Lendell L Jones

O.C. Original Counselor

A question for the provider:

Has someone ever made fun of you and made you feel inadequate or ashamed in your life? _______________

What event happened? _______________
____
____

Do you still sometimes think about it? _______________
____
____

How do you feel now about the event? _______________
____
____

Did you filter it with values or fears? _______________
____
____

Values =
Responsibility

- Accept obligations
- Did the right thing in the situation/ or didn't repeat situation
- Accept accountabilities of your actions

Fears =
Avoid Responsibility

- Lack of positive thinking
- Lack of courage
- Lack of knowledge of what to do

                    Lendell L Jones

How to Build Self-Esteem

Get familiar with your value system

Values. What does that word mean? Values represent what is important to you. Ideally, if something is important to you, you would take care of it, right?

For example:

- Family

- Children

- Health

- Life

- Freedom

- Home

- Job

Be careful not to contradict yourself. How many times have you said that you valued something, only to put alcohol, drugs, or self-defeating behaviors above your words?

Get familiar with setting goals

It is important to set a goal because it gives you something to measure your success by. *Is this goal right for me?* Too often goals are set for other people. Be specific when setting goals.

Don't say, *"I think I'll go back to school and study for a new career."*

Instead say, *"I'm going back to school to study accounting for a new career."*

Is the goal reasonable? Remember, it doesn't matter how small or large the goal is, as long as it's realistic to you.

Self-care

When building self-esteem, it's important to take care of your body (temple). Exercise regularly. Consult your physician and discuss a workout plan.

Healthy Eating Habits

Get to know your foods and the dos and don'ts that will help you to a healthier lifestyle.

Proper hygiene

Nurture yourself daily by taking the necessary steps to maintain your hygiene.

Spirituality

Spirituality plays a major part in building self-esteem. Spirituality is a feeling of calmness and peace. A person doesn't have to be religious to achieve spirituality.

Assertiveness

Allows one to be sure of self; bold when dealing with others.

Honesty

Allows one to be upright and sincere with self and others.

Integrity

Allows one the quality of trustworthiness and being complete.

Sobriety

Abstinence is the ability to be alcohol and drug-free. It's Mission Impossible to be drunk or high and clean and sober at the same time.

Involvement

It's important to stay involved with family, friends, and positive community activities rather than isolating and keeping your good fortunes that are due to sobriety all to yourself.

Acceptance

Admitting the truth when you drink or get high, and about how others and you are affected. Acceptance is the truth for each of you.

The opposite of acceptance is denial. Denial may seem to be the alcohol or drug user's good friend because denial can allow a person to do many things:

1. Allows the alcohol or drug user to assign blame. As long as there is someone or something to blame, the user may not move into acceptance.

2. Allows the alcohol or drug user to create excuses for why they do as they do.

3. Allows the alcohol or drug user to minimize their situation—makes it seem less severe or not as bad as it truly is.

4. Allows the alcohol or drug user to justify their feelings and behaviors.

Remember, getting familiar with your own value system and starting to live by it will increase your self-esteem.

Chapter 14 - Level I, II, and III, the Power of Change

PURPOSE:

To recognize the power of change by understanding intimate self relationships.

GENERAL COMMENTS:

Needs, Wants, and Motivations can lead to positive changes in one's life.

ACTIVITY:

Discuss the concept and fill in the blanks.

114

A question for the provider:

Notes

Have you ever made a change of lifestyle that was hard to do in your life? _______________________

What event happened? _______________________

Do you still sometimes think about it? _______________________

How do you feel now about the event? _______________________

Did you filter it with values or fears? _______________________

Values =

Responsibility

- Accept obligations
- Did the right thing in the situation/ or didn't repeat situation
- Accept accountabilities of your actions

Fears =

Avoid Responsibility

- Lack of positive thinking
- Lack of courage
- Lack of knowledge of what to do

115

Level I, II, and III, the Power of Change:
A Discussion Activity

Write Levels I, II, and III on the board.

- *Level I* needs to be written on the *upper left* side of the board.

- *Level II* needs to be written on the *lower right* side of the board.

- *Level III* needs to be written on the *upper right* side of the board.

- Below Level III write *Recovery*.

Ask the group if they think the discussion of recovery is the ideal place to begin treatment.

After the group has taken a few minutes to share their thoughts on the question you asked, share with the group that discussing recovery isn't always the best place to start. *Why not?* Explain to the group why one should not start with recovery:

1. Some participants may feel they don't have a problem with addiction, and if they don't have a problem with addiction, they have no need to discuss it.

2. Some participants may feel that they have a problem with addiction but do not want to do anything about it.

So instead of starting on Level III, it may be more appropriate to begin on Level I.

Level I: The Self-Contract

Explain that a contract is an agreement between two or more people or parties. A self-contract is an agreement made with one's self. This level is the need. This level gives a clear indication of whether a participant needs to go to the next level. Start Level I by writing on the board:

Negative   *Positive*

Explain to the participants that there are some common statements alcohol and drug users say when describing their self-contracts.

<table>
<tr><th>NEGATIVE</th><th>POSITIVE</th></tr>
<tr><td>I will Drink</td><td>I won't drive</td></tr>
<tr><td>I will Use</td><td>I will limit my usage</td></tr>
<tr><td>I will Drink</td><td>only at home</td></tr>
<tr><td>I will Use</td><td>but not at home</td></tr>
<tr><td>I will Drink</td><td>I will not fight with spouse</td></tr>
<tr><td>I will Use</td><td>I won't go to jail</td></tr>
<tr><td>I will Drink</td><td>It will not interfere with work</td></tr>
<tr><td>I will Use</td><td>I will pay bills</td></tr>
<tr><td>I will Drink</td><td>I won't stay out too late</td></tr>
<tr><td>I will Use</td><td>I will not neglect responsibilities</td></tr>
<tr><td>I will Drink</td><td>I won't let it interfere with my family</td></tr>
</table>

Ask participants if they can identify with any of the examples on the board and let them share their own examples.

Let participants know if they have failed at a single deed on their self-contract, that is an indication that a need for recovery is a possibility.

Tell participants a self-contract is about being honest and real. What is on most self-contracts are promises and words they've told themselves many times before.

For example: How many times have you told yourself, when I use, I will do this or I won't do that, though eventually you find yourself going against your words?

Level II: Having a Desire

This is the *"want"* level. It gives a clear indication of whether a participant wants to go to the next level.

Ask participants to answer the question, *"How will I benefit by not using?"*

Explain to participants that there are some common statements alcohol and drug users say before they are asked how they will benefit:

- I won't get a DUI
- I will have better family relationships
- I will be less likely to have legal problems
- I will be more responsible
- I will probably be home more

- I will have a better work relationship
- I will have better health
- I will be more involved with my children
- I will manage my finances better
- I will have better social relationships

Ask participants if they can identify with any of the examples on the board and whether they would like to share their own examples.

Let participants know by understanding and identifying with Level I and Level II, that they can then move on to Level III.

Level III: Recovery

This is the working level—the action.

Write on the board, under Recovery the basic H.O.W. formula:

*H*onesty.
Ask participants, *"How has your usage been problematic for others?"*

*O*pen-mindedness.
Ask participants, *"What part has your usage played in your recent problems?"*

*W*illingness.
Ask participants to describe a treatment plan to improve their situation.

Then write, ***Change*** on the board and ask participants,

"What must come first before any change can begin?"

Answer: There must be a reason before any change occurs. Why do I want to change? What is the reason?

Ask participants,

"If there's a good reason to change, does that mean that change will automatically occur?

Answer: No, let participants know they may have the best intentions in the world for change and still change may not occur.

Reason + Motivation = Change

When a reason is identified, the participant must then be motivated to do whatever is in their power to make change occur.

Reason + Motivation = Change

Share examples with participants on some possible reasons for change:

• Better health	• Better social involvement
• Better family relationships	• Better financial status
• Better self-esteem	• Better job performance
• Better parenting	• Better chance to obtain freedom

Once participants have found a reason to change, they must then be motivated to change.

So before participants even begin to discuss recovery, sometimes they first need to be clear on their needs and wants.

Chapter 15 - Delli Dells's Story

PURPOSE:

Follow the dynamics of Delli Dell as he comes to terms with how his choices are affecting his behaviors and outcome.

GENERAL COMMENTS:

Optional strategies for facilitators:

1. Have participants read the story individually and then process it with the group.

2. Have participants go around the group table or circle and each one read a paragraph and process with the group.

3. Have participants separate into groups and have the chosen person read the story to the individual group. The individual groups will discuss the story before coming back to the group as a whole and then process.

4. Facilitator reads the story to the group and then allows the group to process.

ACTIVITY:

Facilitator will have participants read Delli Dell's Story and process the events of his story.

Lendell L Jones

O.C. Original Counselor

A question for the provider:

Notes

Have you ever taken your frustrations out on loved ones in your life? _______________________________________

What event happened? _______________________________
____
____

Do you still sometimes think about it? _________________
____
____

How do you feel now about the event? _________________
____
____

Did you filter it with values or fears? _________________
____
____

Values =

Responsibility

- Accept obligations
- Did the right thing in the situation/ or didn't repeat situation
- Accept accountabilities of your actions

Fears =

Avoid Responsibility

- Lack of positive thinking
- Lack of courage
- Lack of knowledge of what to do

121

Delli Dell's Story

She always complains about everything I do. It seems as if I can't do anything right in her eyes. I really try to be patient but the more she nags me, I don't know what happens. All I do know is I become so frustrated and boom! The fight is on. I must admit, I feel very inadequate whenever she questions my parenting skills. I know I'm not the perfect father, but why can't she see I'm trying! I mean, I never had a father to teach me about the trials of life, so what makes her think I should be an expert at it?

I'm not a dope. I fully understand what it means to be the quarterback of my family. I accept that leadership. But doesn't the quarterback need help from the rest of the players to make a team successful? I'm the one who has to fix what is broken around here. I upkeep the yard, and I'm the one who does most of the cleaning in the house. Yet, no matter what I do, my wife seems to complain, and most of the time it's about money.

It's not that I don't want to do physical activities with my children, but living with a disability sometimes makes tasks that appear simple for most people extremely hard for me. My children can't seem to understand that being on disability, I can't afford to buy them expensive clothing and toys, and all the other things they complain about not having. If other kids' parents have money to spend like that, good for them. I don't! Does my family think I like being like this?

What really drives me bats is when my wife continues to talk about how she wishes our relationship was healthier. I have no idea what her view of a "healthy" relationship looks like. As far as I am concerned, there is no such thing as a healthy relationship and people who claim to be in one are fakers and hypocrites. You know the part that really gets me? Up until my disability, we seemed to have functioned quite well as a family. We took the good with the bad and none of us pretended to be perfect. Now, all of sudden, it is so important for her to live in this fictional, healthy relationship world. I also realize if I want to keep my relationship going with my family, I need to figure out how to handle situations that frustrate me differently.

Sometimes, of course, I gamble away what little money I do have and that infuriates my wife. I can't tell you how many times our utilities have been turned off due to me losing my check by gambling. The point is gambling allows me time away from the house and away from the nagging wife and complaining children. If I had more support from my family, I think I'll be a better gambler. It's something about intuition. I'm just so close to hitting the jackpot and if I do I bet, my family will support me then. Don't get me wrong. I don't gamble off all my money.

I do have my gambling under control. Just two weeks ago, I took $100 out of the house payment, went gambling, and wound up bringing $250 back home. So that proves I don't have a real problem with gambling because if I did, I would continue gambling and lose it all, right? So if you really think about it, my problem isn't gambling, my problem is the pressure the world has placed on me.

Chapter 16 - 1st and Goal

PURPOSE:

To promote growth by using critical thinking and a self-measure movement method regarding a map to increase responsibility.

GENERAL COMMENTS:

Understanding the odds to be successful can be a motivator.

ACTIVITY:

Discussion and fill in the blanks.

124

A question for the provider:

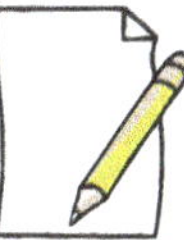

Have you experienced or at least thought you were on top of the world in your life? _______________________________

What event happened? _______________________________

Do you still sometimes think about it? _______________________

How do you feel now about the event? _______________________

Did you filter it with values or fears? _______________________

Values =

Responsibility

- Accept obligations
- Did the right thing in the situation/ or didn't repeat situation
- Accept accountabilities of your actions

Fears =

Avoid Responsibility

- Lack of positive thinking
- Lack of courage
- Lack of knowledge of what to do

125

1st and Goal

1. Write "1st and Goal" on the board.

2. Write "11 Xs and 11 0s" on the board.

3. Explain Xs represent defense and 0s represent offense.

4. Explain that the defense is trying to push through and sack the quarterback and keep the participant from moving forward into the end zone.

5. Write "Goal" on each side of the board.

6. The offense has two goals: the first goal is to protect the quarterback and the second goal is to move the ball into the end zone.

7. Explain to participants that the beginning of recovery is the time to <u>identify something important enough to them that they are willing to protect it.</u> Once they are stable enough to manage that, then it's time to make plans on moving forward and to make their wants and needs in life a reality.

8. Write "Reinforcement" on the four corners of the playing field and draw three rows of four circles beneath each reinforcement.

9. Explain to them the reinforcements represent the fans of the game and the people of the world that they come in contact with daily.

10. Reinforcement will be either of the two. They will be positive or they will be negative. One will be there to cheer on the defenses to stop participants from reaching their goals, and the other will be there as a supporter and to assist whenever possible to help participants reach their goals.

1ˢᵀ AND GOAL

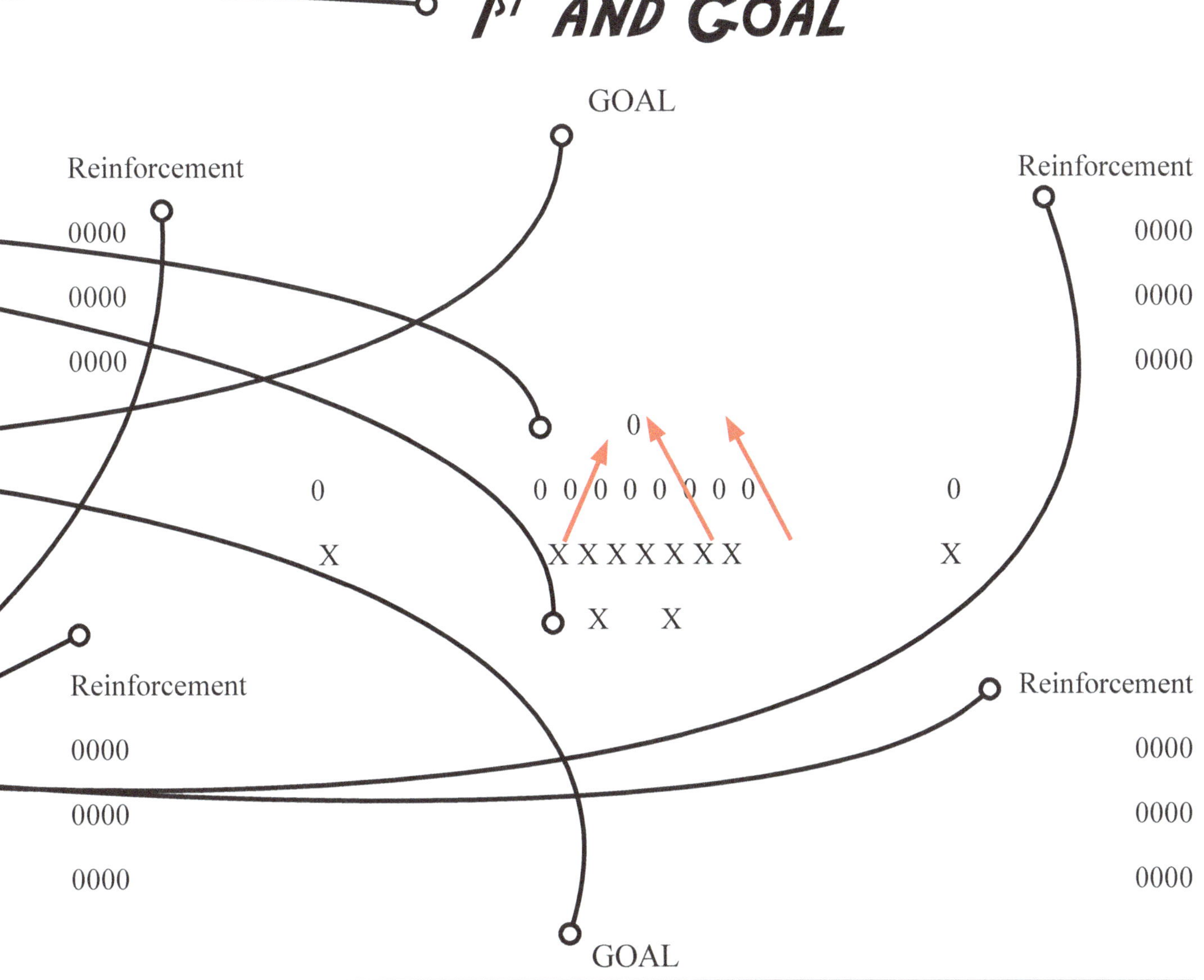

Reinforcements will either be: _____Positive_____ or _____Negative_____ influences in your life.

To read the defense and move the ball, participants must be able to recognize their own self-defeating behaviors:

[ ]	Anger	[ ]	Hurt
[ ]	Low self-esteem	[ ]	Doubt
[ ]	Fear	[ ]	Resentments
[ ]	Shame	[ ]	Insecurities
[ ]	Guilt	[ ]	Past failures
[ ]	Laziness		

Chapter 17 - Peaceful Fighting Amongst Partners

PURPOSE:

To improve coexisting relationships by recognizing the strengths and limitations in supportive relationships.

GENERAL COMMENTS:

Establishing healthy boundaries without discriminating against others and letting go of old ways of thinking and behaving.

ACTIVITY:

- Discuss Peaceful Fighting as a group or with individual participants.

- Ask participants if they have anything to add.

- Allow participants to share their direct or indirect experiences with Peaceful Fighting.

128

A question for the provider:

Notes

Have you ever had the desire to whup your partner's butt in your life? _______________________________

What event happened? _______________________________
____
____

Do you still sometimes think about it? _______________________________
____
____

How do you feel now about the event? _______________________________
____
____

Did you filter it with values or fears? _______________________________
____
____

Values =

Responsibility

- Accept obligations
- Did the right thing in the situation/ or didn't repeat situation
- Accept accountabilities of your actions

Fears =

Avoid Responsibility

- Lack of positive thinking
- Lack of courage
- Lack of knowledge of what to do

Peaceful Fighting Amongst Partners

Partners should never argue. The goal is to learn how to debate during disagreeable times.

When eye-to-eye differences surface during your relationship, as they inevitably will, partners should allow each other a minimum of two minutes at a time to openly plead their case.

Both partners are strongly recommended to be open-minded and aware of their opposite views and angle as well as their own views and angle.

Example:

Partner 1: Has a wide imagination, probable research, is mild-mannered and ultimately has a strong desire to be fair.

Partner 2: Uses knowledge and educated guesses. They're fair, strong-willed, caring, and trustworthy.

It is critical that both partners empower themselves with debating skills. These skills are accomplished by demonstrating:

- Respect

- Trustworthiness

- Friendship

Respect your partner's strengths, weaknesses, and ideas. Trust that your partner has yours and their best interest at heart. Be the type of friend you would like to have.

1. Never bring children or other family members into the debate to gain the upper lever with low blows.

2. While debating, neither partner should use sarcasm or attacking words.

3. While debating, partners should give it their best to get their point across.

4. However, in defeat, acknowledge your partner's point and go out as a mature person.

> **Learning** *how to debate your wants and needs in a healthy way sets a prime example to your children and others.*

When we fight fair, everyone has a chance to win.

1. We're less likely to become angry about the current situation.

2. We can keep our cool without feeling like a fool.

3. We can be at peace with our partner without carrying resentment.

4. The rest of the day with our partner is more likely to be pleasant.

5. Most importantly, we proved to ourselves and our partner that we can disagree without thinking it's the end of the world.

NO DEBATE BETWEEN PARTNERS SHOULD LAST MORE THAN 30 MINUTES—PERIOD.

So, you still want to fight? Bring it on! Just remember you better fight fair.

Chapter 18 - Tools for Parents

PURPOSE:

To identify some logical consequences that will help children to be more willing to cooperate in their upbringing.

GENERAL COMMENTS:

Participating in decision-making gives children a sense of their own worth.

ACTIVITY:

1. Discuss Tools for Parents as a group or with individual participants.

2. Ask participants if they have anything to add.

3. Allow participants to share their direct or indirect experiences with the topic.

4. Complete the worksheet.

132

A question for the provider:

Notes

Have you ever felt insecure in your parenting skills in your life? _______________________

What event happened? _______________________

Do you still sometimes think about it? _______________________

How do you feel now about the event? _______________________

Did you filter it with values or fears? _______________________

Values =
Responsibility

- Accept obligations
- Did the right thing in the situation/ or didn't repeat situation
- Accept accountabilities of your actions

Fears =
Avoid Responsibility

- Lack of positive thinking
- Lack of courage
- Lack of knowledge of what to do

133

Tools for Parents

1. Parents may strengthen their relationship with their children by giving clear and precise expectations of what they're seeking. It is absolutely imperative to give consequences and rewards for the expectations.

Write an example of a clear and precise expectation that you are willing to present to any of your children at this time. ________________________________
____
____

What would you consider to be an appropriate consequence and reward for your expectation?
Consequence ____
____
Reward ____
____

2. Parents may strengthen their relationship with their children by following through with what they say. This gives a clear message that the parent is reliable and stable.

Write an example of a time when you did not follow through on what you said. ____________
____
____

What was the result? ____
____
____

Write an example of a time when it was hard to do, yet you did follow through with what you said. ____
____
____

What were the results? _______________________________________

____

3. Parents can strengthen their relationships with their children by being consistent with the rules they have set.

What has made enforcing rules on your children difficult? _______________

____

____

As a child, how accepting were you toward rules? _______________

____

____

As an adult, how accepting are you toward rules? _______________

____

____

Why do you think it is important to follow rules? _______________

____

____

4. Parents may strengthen their relationship with their children by weathering the storm. Children do not always like change and will challenge parental stability.

What plan would you enforce to defend against your child begging, pleading, bargaining, crying, manipulating, arguing, and fighting to get their way? _______________

____

____

5. Parents can strengthen their relationship with children by understanding the importance of positive affirmations. Remember that negative consequences do not always get children to respond. Positive benefits, for the most part, stimulate children. (Bees are attracted to honey not, flyswatters.)

What are five things you think your children do well?

(1) ____

(2) ____

(3) ____

(4) ____

(5) ____

What are five things you think you do well?

(1) ____

(2) ____

(3) ____

(4) ____

(5) ____

Chapter 19 - Three Commonly Used Parenting Skills

PURPOSE:

To identify what makes a parent and which responsibilities a parent needs to attain.

GENERAL COMMENTS:

An ideal parent is often described as a comfortable parent where a sense of order presides.

ACTIVITY:

Discussion and fill in the blanks.

Lendell L Jones

O.C. Original Counselor

A question for the provider:

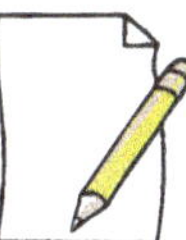

Notes

Have you ever felt extremely confident with your parenting skills in your life? _______________________

What event happened? _______________________

Do you still sometimes think about it? _______________________

How do you feel now about the event? _______________________

Did you filter it with values or fears? _______________________

Values =

Responsibility

- Accept obligations
- Did the right thing in the situation/ or didn't repeat situation
- Accept accountabilities of your actions

Fears =

Avoid Responsibility

- Lack of positive thinking
- Lack of courage
- Lack of knowledge of what to do

139

Lendell L Jones

Three Commonly Used Parenting Skills

Autocratic -

Governed by one parent with unlimited control (my way or no way, do as I say not as I do). Much of the time these types of parents manipulate and control their children's life because their own life is inadequate and limited.

Permissive -

This type of parenting allows their children to do poor in school and supplies an unhealthy structure. This parent often manipulates their children by making the children feel sorry for them. (playing the victim role). Children with this type of parent usually grow up without learning how to adjust as an adult. They often find themselves in dysfunctional relationships, have a hard time keeping proper employment, go to jail at least once during their lifetime, and pass these learned behaviors on to their children.

Authoritative -

This parent sets healthy boundaries and rules for their children. They encourage their children to succeed. They empower their children to follow through with responsibilities. This parent sets an example of what is expected from their children.

Duties of a Responsible Parent

- According to Lendell L. Jones

I realize that in today's culture, it is extremely hard to rear children in a secular society with all the distractions the culture has placed as values. I deeply empathize with all parents because as a parent myself I understand the challenges of parenting. However, the fact of the matter is, when I made the conscious decision to become a parent, my top priority at that moment was to rear my children and coach them into becoming responsible adults. I must stay alert to the fact that most children do only as much as their parents enforce them to do. Children are not born with an Instruction to Life book. So as a loving and caring parent, I dedicate my life to coaching my children into adulthood. It has been written, "Teach a child what to do when they're young and they will know what to do when they are older."

All I want for my children, (as a primary physical custodial parent, with absolute understanding that it will be my responsibility to take care of these basic needs for my children) is that they assume the following:

- Make sure they keep at least a C-point grade average in school at all times. This means I may have to use all resources I know and then sometimes I may have to stay up until three in the morning making sure their homework is completed. I may have to run them all over town to private schools and tutors. Believe me, most parents don't like to do these things but responsible parents know that it's necessary for their children's success. No parent can righteously blame their child for failing at school. This may sound harsh but it is true. Children don't fail! Irresponsible parenting skills fail children. As a parent, I must remind myself that if I don't know how to teach my children, my responsibility is to search out resources and learn how, or find the right people who know how to teach them. A child failing at school should not be an option for any parent.

- Make sure that they are involved in at least one extra activity; this may include sports, music, dance, etc. This builds self-esteem, character, and team-building skills. Not only is this important for the child, but it's also important for children to witness their parent's involvement in what they are doing. Parents need to be their children's strongest support system.

- My children are very involved with their church. They go to Sunday School every Sunday. Not only is Ideal Baptist Church good for their spiritual well-being, but it also allows them to fellowship with their African American peers and learn more about their culture. Parents must understand, a child may grow up and never attend church again but it's important to introduce and teach them biblical understandings while they're young.

- Make sure they are involved in an exercise plan every day at home. I will have them exercise for at least thirty minutes a day. I will let their mother know the exercise plan so she can hold the children to it when they are with her. This is important not only for their health but it builds structure. It's great that they exercise at school and run around and play at home, but that should not exclude a structural exercise program.

- Make sure they are safe from alcohol, drug, and tobacco environments. I'm not saying people should not do these things; however, research has shown us that children who are brought up in these types of settings have a greater chance of mirroring these behaviors than children who were not.

Parents, please don't let this agenda scare you. Odds are strongly on your side that your children will not come to you as an adult and say:

"Mom and Dad,

I hate you for forcing me to do well in school when I was younger. I hate you for getting me involved with activities that developed into a skill or talent. I hate you for rearing me in an alcohol, drug, and tobacco-free setting. I hate you for making me get up off that couch and exercise. I hate you for helping me understand the importance of biblical teachings."

Am I capable and willing to provide these basic needs for my children?

Yes__________ I have adequate stability in my life.

No _________ I do not have adequate stability in my life. Why? ___________________________

____

____

Parent:____

Date :____

May 19, 2012

Dear Shylisa,

I know at times life seems difficult, painful and giving up appears to be much easier than pushing through but no matter what this world put you through I pray you will always remember this: You're here not by chance, but by God's choosing, his hands formed you and made you the person you are. He compares you to no one else; you are one of a kind. You lack nothing that his Grace can't give you. He has allowed you to be here at this time in history to fulfill His special purpose for this generation. Shylisa I strongly encourage you to trust and believe in yourself and with God's blessings all things are possible. As you already know, this world sometime is mean and cruel but please don't let this world or anyone keep you from being the person God created. You are special and I love you from the center of my heart, my love for you will always remain. True dat! I know sometimes we have bad communication blocks but I sincerely want you to be sure of one thing, your dad will not give up on trying communicating better with you. The truth is we may be working on improving our communicating skills for the rest of our lives. I have found it comfortable to justify my communication blocks by saying I'm trying to help or teach you. The truth is I'm scared to death that you may get hurt or fail. Thankfully Steven my counselor is helping me to let go a little and allow you to make some decisions for yourself. I must admit it's going to be hard for me but I'm willing to loosen up. Shylisa I also realize I push you to do well in school and my dearest daughter that may never change. But I do want you to know, you are a 100 times more important to me than any grade you could ever make. The good news for you is, as smart as your dad is and how rich he's going to be, you don't need school or a job you can live off his money for the rest of your life. SHYLISA: AND IF YOU BUY THAT--- I HAVE SOME OCEAN FRONT PROPERTY IN ARIZONA also. Just kidding but I do want you to know I love you so much!

Love,

Dad

Chapter 20 - Tips on Parenting

PURPOSE:

To discover new tips to strengthen the relationship between children and parents.

GENERAL COMMENTS:

Parents can better understand children's behaviors by understanding their underlying temperament.

ACTIVITY:

1. Discuss Tips on Parenting as a group or with individual participants.

2. Ask participants if they have anything to add.

3. Allow participants to share their direct or indirect experiences with Tips on Parenting.

144

A question for the provider:

Have you ever experienced serious regrets about something you did as a parent in your life? ______________________

What event happened? ______________________

Do you still sometimes think about it? ______________________

How do you feel now about the event? ______________________

Did you filter it with values or fears? ______________________

Values =

Responsibility

- Accept obligations
- Did the right thing in the situation/ or didn't repeat situation
- Accept accountabilities of your actions

Fears =

Avoid Responsibility

- Lack of positive thinking
- Lack of courage
- Lack of knowledge of what to do

145

Tips on Parenting

1. Recognize your child's temperament: Is he/she flexible or easily adaptable to people, situations, and changes rather quickly? Is he/she feisty or difficult? Does he/she have a hard time adapting to new situations and often becomes loud, unpleasant, or disagreeable when things don't go his/her way? Is he/she fearful? Does he/she appear to be shy or have discomfort with new situations and adapt slowly and with caution? Differences in children's temperaments are normal. The key to understanding a child's particular trait which can influence their behavior is to discover ways to handle it as a teaching tool.

2. Share time with your children. Schedule a date day or night and share time alone. This could be an opportunity to demonstrate to your child what respectful dating is.

3. Be patient. We as parents are old dogs. We have a lifetime of experience and hard knocks, mistakes, or regrets. Our battle scars have taught us well. Children will also discover their own unique battles.

4. Become involved with what is important in your child's life and not just what you may think is important for them.

5. Stay on topic. This can be another tool for demonstrating the value of being focused on your child.

6. Be responsible for your own behaviors. Parents, be accountable: admit when you made a mistake, follow through on promises, and live as an example of a responsible adult and parent.

7. Encourage your child to try new, positive, and challenging projects (sports, music, a class, etc.).

8. Accept your child's growth and changes. Learn to become flexible to your growing child's needs.

9. Send messages to your children that you have faith in them and support their efforts. Purposely include them in meaningful conversations.

10. Be both firm and kind. Talk less and act more. Give clear expectations and logical consequences.

There are generally five characteristics that describe a child's temperament:

1. Activity level

2. Emotional intensity

3. Frustration tolerance

4. Reaction to change

5. Reaction to new people

There is no right or wrong, better or worse temperament. Every child is born with their own way to approach the world.

Remember, the goal isn't to change your child's temperament, but to focus on their contribution, assets, and strength to help them feel adequate. You can do this by using phrases like:

- I love . . . (you, what you do, what you should do).

- I'm listening . . . (to what you're saying).

- I want to understand, please help me . . . (understand what you're talking about).

Chapter 21 - Quarterbacking the Family

PURPOSE:

To identify some of the beliefs and behavioral patterns that can have long-lasting effects on children.

GENERAL COMMENTS:

Parenting at times can be an unpopular and difficult task. When one fulfills responsibilities, there is a sense of accomplishment.

ACTIVITY:

1. Discuss Quarterbacking the Family as a group or with individual participants.

2. Ask participants if they have anything to add.

3. Allow participants to share their direct or indirect experiences with Quarterbacking the Family.

148

A question for the provider:

Notes

Have you ever felt unsure of how to lead your family in your life? ________________

What event happened? ________________

Do you still sometimes think about it? ________________

How do you feel now about the event? ________________

Did you filter it with values or fears? ________________

Values =

Responsibility

- Accept obligations
- Did the right thing in the situation/ or didn't repeat situation
- Accept accountabilities of your actions

Fears =

Avoid Responsibility

- Lack of positive thinking
- Lack of courage
- Lack of knowledge of what to do

149

Lendell L Jones

Quarterbacking the Family

According to Lendell L. Jones

1. Parents, trust your instincts. If you are experiencing feelings that something is not right with a family member, encouraged that family member to talk about it.

2. Parents, don't feel that you have to solve all your family members' problems. Sometimes the best practice is to listen to them.

3. Parents, always remember that being a parent is more valuable than being a friend. Friendship is an added bonus for you being a successful parent.

4. Parents, allow yourself to try new things with family members. Don't get caught up in 'this is the way it's always been.'

5. Parents, it's not your responsibility to keep your family members happy and honorable. However, it is your responsibility to mirror how to be happy and honorable.

6. Parents, you don't always have to be right. Be open to your family members' points of view.

7. Parents are encouraged to be open and share with family members their life experiences about similar situations and challenges that their family members are experiencing.

8. Parents should always make clear to family members that they have their best interests at heart.

9. Parents' primary position is to lead fair and just. To give unselfishly and discipline firmly and righteously.

10. Parents should let family members know it's okay to feel their feelings and they may not know why or what the family member is going through.

11. Parents are encouraged not to compare family members to others. Everyone is his/her own unique person.

12. Parents should always allow space for mistakes. When family members make mistakes, that ensures parents that their family member isn't perfect and has room to grow. Parents can be part of that growth.

Chapter 22 - Living with a Disability

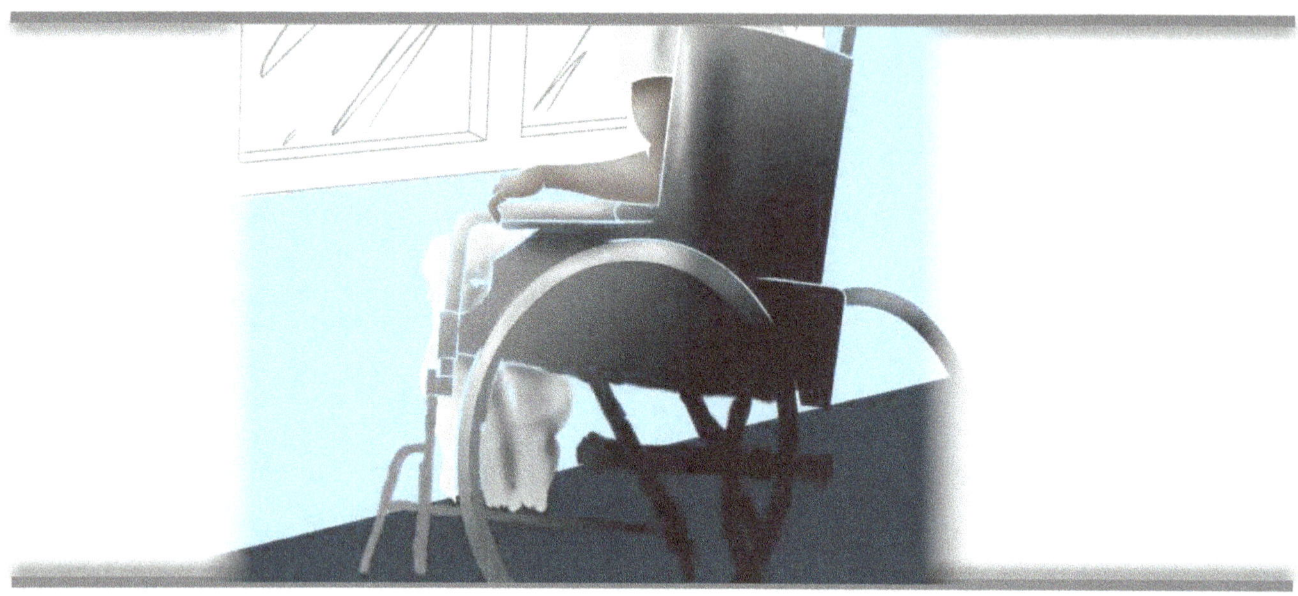

PURPOSE:

To increase knowledge and awareness about individuals that live with a disability.

GENERAL COMMENTS:

Acknowledging positive qualities in others can enhance and establish a better relationship.

ACTIVITY:

1. Discuss Living with a Disability as a group or with individual participants.

2. Ask participants if they have anything to add.

3. Allow participants to share their direct or indirect experiences with Living with a Disability.

152

Have you or a family member experienced an emotional, mental, or physical disability in your life? _______________

What event happened? ___________________________
____
____

Do you still sometimes think about it? _______________
____
____

How do you feel now about the event? _______________
____
____

Did you filter it with values or fears? ________________
____
____

Values =
Responsibility

- Accept obligations
- Did the right thing in the situation/ or didn't repeat situation
- Accept accountabilities of your actions

Fears =
Avoid Responsibility

- Lack of positive thinking
- Lack of courage
- Lack of knowledge of what to do

Living with a Disability

A disability is a condition that impairs a person to do relatively normal tasks. It may include various types of chronic disease, intellectual impairment, sensory impairment, and/or physical impairment. Disability is conceptualized as being a multidimensional experience for the person involved. There may be effects on organs or body parts and there may be effects on a person's participation in different areas of life. Correspondingly, three dimensions of disability are recognized as: body structure and function (and impairment thereof), activity (and activity restrictions), and participation (and participation restrictions). The classification also recognizes the role of physical and socio-environmental factors in affecting disability outcomes.

Types of Disabilities

Types of disabilities include various physical and mental impairments that can impede or reduce a person's ability to carry out his/her daily activities. These impairments can be termed as a disability of the person to do his/her daily activities. These impairments can be termed as a disability to do his/her daily activities. "Disability" can be broken down into a number of broad sub-categories, which include the following:

Mobility and Physical Impairments
This category of disability includes people with varying types of physical disabilities including:

- Upper limb(s) disability

- Lower limb(s) disability

- Manual dexterity

- Disability in coordination with different organs of the body

Disability in mobility: can be either in-born or acquired with age problems. It could also be the effect of a disease. People who have a broken bone also fall into this category of disability.

Spinal Cord Disability
Spinal cord injury can sometimes lead to lifelong disabilities. This kind of injury mostly occurs

due to severe accidents. The injury can be either complete or incomplete. In an incomplete injury, the messages conveyed by the spinal cord are not completely lost whereas a complete injury results in total dysfunctioning of the sensory organs. In some cases, spinal cord disability can be a birth defect.

Head Injuries - Brain Disability

A disability in the brain occurs due to a brain injury. The magnitude of the brain injury can range from mild to moderate or severe. There are two types of brain injuries:

1. Acquired Brain Injury (ABI)

2. Traumatic Brain Injury (TBI)

ABI is not a hereditary defect but is the degeneration that occurs after birth. The causes of such cases of injury are many and are mainly due to external forces applied to the body parts. TBI results in emotional dysfunction and behavioral disturbance.

Vision Disability

There are hundreds of thousands of people that suffer from minor to serious vision disabilities or impairments. These injuries can also result in some serious problems or diseases like blindness and ocular trauma, to name a few. Some of the common vision impairments include scratched corneas, scratches on the sclera, diabetes-related eye conditions, dry eyes, and corneal grafts.

Hearing Disability

Hearing disabilities include people that are completely or partially deaf.

People who are partially deaf can often use hearing aids to assist their hearing. Deafness can be evident at birth or occur later in life from several biologic causes, such as meningitis which can damage the auditory organs or the cochlea. Deaf people use sign language as a means of communication. Hundreds of sign languages are in use around the world. In linguistic terms, sign languages are as rich and complex as any oral language, despite the common misconception that they are not "real languages."

Cognitive or Learning Disabilities

Cognitive disabilities are types of impairments presented in people who are suffering from dyslexia and various other learning difficulties including speech disorders.

Psychological Disorders

Affective Disorders: Disorders of mood or feeling states either short or long-term. Mental Impairment is the term used to describe people who have experienced psychiatric problems or illnesses such as Personality Disorders. A personality disorder is defined as deeply inadequate patterns of behavior and thought of sufficient severity to cause significant impairment to daily activities.

Schizophrenia:

A mental disorder characterized by disturbances of thinking, mood, and behavior.

Invisible Disabilities

Invisible disabilities are disabilities that are not immediately apparent to others. It is estimated that 10% of people in the U.S. have a medical condition considered a type of invisible disability.

Chapter 23 - Guest Speaker

PURPOSE:

To give participants a view of what life can be like when not using.

GENERAL COMMENTS:

Recovering addict will share their story from the fall to the come-up.

ACTIVITY:

Ask questions and gather information about support group communities and resources.

158

Notes

Values =

Responsibility

- Accept obligations
- Did the right thing in the situation/ or didn't repeat situation
- Accept accountabilities of your actions

Fears =

Avoid Responsibility

- Lack of positive thinking
- Lack of courage
- Lack of knowledge of what to do

159

Chapter 24 - Healthy Relationships

PURPOSE:

To strengthen relationships by understanding and developing healthy boundaries.

GENERAL COMMENTS:

Setting healthy boundaries will increase self-esteem which can lead to better relationships.

ACTIVITY:

1. Discuss Healthy Relationships as a group or with individual participants.

2. Ask participants if they have anything to add.

3. Allow participants to share their direct or indirect experiences with Healthy Relationships.

4. Fill in the blanks.

160

A question for the provider:

Notes

Have you ever stayed in a relationship longer than you should have in your life? _______________________________

What event happened? _______________________________

Do you still sometimes think about it? _______________________________

How do you feel now about the event? _______________________________

Did you filter it with values or fears? _______________________________

Values =

Responsibility

- Accept obligations
- Did the right thing in the situation/ or didn't repeat situation
- Accept accountabilities of your actions

Fears =

Avoid Responsibility

- Lack of positive thinking
- Lack of courage
- Lack of knowledge of what to do

161

Healthy Relationships

Question: What is a relationship?

Answer: A logical or natural association between two or more people.

Draw two circles on the discussion marker board (chalkboard). Ask participants to draw circles above columns A and B.

By looking at the two circles on top of columns A and B, are you able to tell which circle is healthy and which is dysfunctional?

Keep in mind that there's a thin line between a healthy and a dysfunctional relationship.

Although much of the time both relationships are made from the same traits, these traits are important in all relationships.

The challenge may be, are you using these traits in a healthy or dysfunctional manner?

Columns A and B will provide examples of how these traits resemble the same, but the outcome of behaviors are opposite.

In a healthy relationship, knowing your strength and limitations, along with setting boundaries according to your values, is priority.

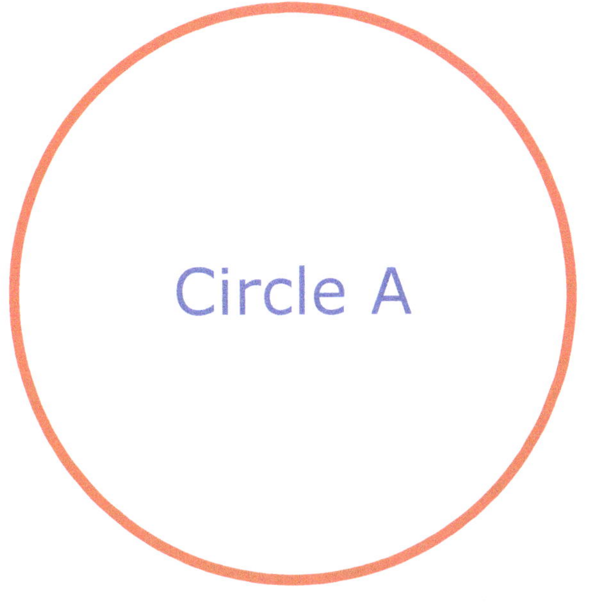

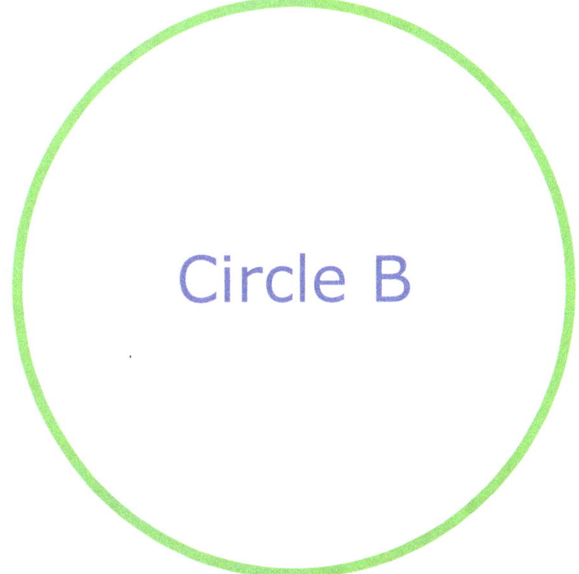

<table>
<tr><td>

Circle A

- I trust you blindly without boundaries.

- I allow fear to manipulate me and control my emotions.

- I honestly feel unsafe to share my feelings with you.

- I think I respect you, but demonstrate little respect for myself. That's why I allow you to continue hurting me.

- I use much energy to control others' behaviors.

- I'm open to hearing only what I want to and I make quick decisions.

</td><td>

Circle B

- I trust you, along with setting my own, healthy boundaries.

- I allow myself to feel fear without resorting to fighting or going into fight mode.

- I am honest with my feelings and share them openly with you.

- I respect you as well as myself and others by demonstrating my values.

- I control my own feelings and behaviors and understand that I have little control over others.

- I'm open to listening to your point of view before I make a decision.

</td></tr>
</table>

Chapter 25 - Praising Relationships

PURPOSE:

To strengthen relationships by understanding the power of honoring your partner's boundaries.

GENERAL COMMENTS:

Learning to praise and set healthy boundaries can strengthen relationships.

ACTIVITY:

1. Discuss Praising Relationships as a group or with individual participants.

2. Ask participants if they have anything to add.

3. Allow participants to share their direct or indirect experiences with Praising Relationships.

4. Discuss and fill in the blanks.

A question for the provider:

Notes

Have you ever been treated extremely well during a relationship in your life? _______________

What event happened? _______________

Do you still sometimes think about it? _______________

How do you feel now about the event? _______________

Did you filter it with values or fears? _______________

Values =
Responsibility

- Accept obligations
- Did the right thing in the situation/ or didn't repeat situation
- Accept accountabilities of your actions

Fears =
Avoid Responsibility

- Lack of positive thinking
- Lack of courage
- Lack of knowledge of what to do

165

Praising Relationships

Praising is essential to any healthy relationship. Too often, partners do not receive the praise they deserve. Many times, the importance of praising is not realized and the lacking of praising can weaken relationships. There are many ways of praising. Here are a few examples:

- Help your partner feel good about themselves.

- Acknowledge your partner's efforts.

- Comfort your partner during stressful situations.

- Acknowledge your partner's importance to you.

- Express your desire to continue dating your partner.

Rule of thumb:

When praises are specific and genuine, they generally have the best impact on relationships. Praises that are vague may seem unsupported and can send mixed messages that are confusing to your partner.

Treat your partner like they're single and you're trying to earn their heart and affection for the first time.

Remember to be romantic. True romance involves action to express affection in a meaningful way.

Keep your sex life invigorated. Kiss your partner in the morning like you don't want them to leave. Suggest new ideas; be willing to put your partner's pleasures ahead of your own. Let your partner know they mean much more to you than sex.

Become a helpmate. Help out with the cooking and household duties. Stay involved with the children. No one is a Super Person. Everyone can use some help.

Continue to communicate. Talk with your partner. Ask how their day went. Share about your day. Ask questions that you really want to know about. Talk to them in a way that lets them know that they are the most important person in the world to you. Make sure you are actually listening to what your partner is saying.

Surprise gifts. In healthy relationships, partners are special every day, not only on special occasions. Surprise your partner with a special gift for no special reason other than they are special to you.

When should you praise your partner? _______________________________________
____
____

Why should you praise your partner? _______________________________________
____
____

How should you praise your partner? _______________________________________
____
____

Do your part.
Don't put your partner under pressure to ask you to pull your own weight. This can make your partner feel like a nag and can create an adult/child relationship. Your partner is not your father/mother. They're your equal.

Chapter 26 - Gambling

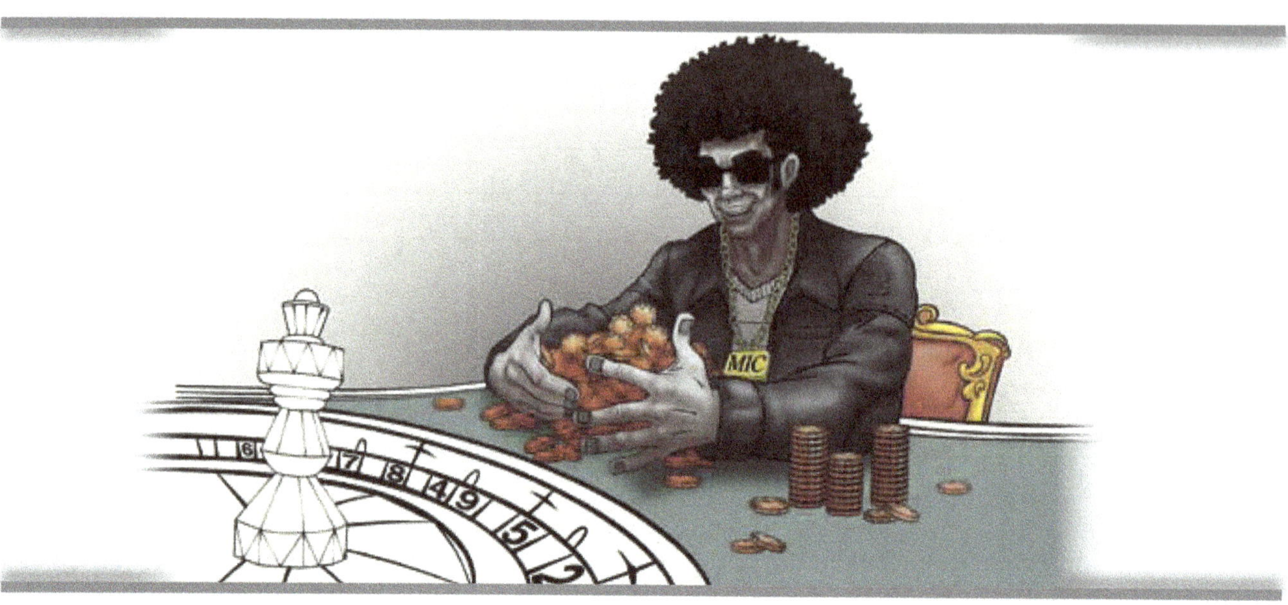

PURPOSE:

To increase knowledge and awareness about the possible dangers of gambling.

GENERAL COMMENTS:

Gambling behaviors have been known to affect family relationships just as alcohol and drugs do. Inform participants that this program was written many years ago and invite them to research modern-day statistics.

ACTIVITY:

1. Discuss Gambling as a group or with individual participants.

2. Ask participants if they have anything to add.

3. Allow participants to share their direct or indirect experiences with Gambling.

168

A question for the provider:

Have you ever placed yourself in a high-risk situation in your life? _______________________________

What event happened? _______________________________

Do you still sometimes think about it? _______________________________

How do you feel now about the event? _______________________________

Did you filter it with values or fears? _______________________________

Values =

Responsibility

- Accept obligations
- Did the right thing in the situation/ or didn't repeat situation
- Accept accountabilities of your actions

Fears =

Avoid Responsibility

- Lack of positive thinking
- Lack of courage
- Lack of knowledge of what to do

169

Gambling

Problems with gambling can strain your relationships, interfere with responsibilities at home and work, and lead to financial catastrophe. You may even do things you never thought you would like stealing to get money to gamble or taking money meant for your children. You may think you can't stop, but problem gambling and gambling addiction are treatable. If you're ready to admit you have a problem and seek help, you can overcome your gambling problem and regain control of your life.

Gambling addiction, also known as compulsive gambling disorder, may start quietly, but over time it takes over a person's ability to control the urge to gamble. A person may have a gambling problem if it causes disruption in any major part of their life: psychological, physical, social, or vocational. Gambling is a serious problem if it interferes with finances, relationships, or work.

Signs of Progressive Gambling Addiction:

1. An increasing preoccupation with gambling. Have frequent thoughts about gambling experiences.

2. Tolerance. Need to bet larger or more frequent wagers to experience the same "high or thrill."

3. Irritability or restlessness associated with attempts to stop gambling.

4. Gambling has become a source or outlet to escape problems.

5. Chasing losses. Trying to win back losses with more gambling.

6. Lying to family, friends, and employers to hide the extent of gambling habits.

7. Loss of control. Unsuccessfully attempting to stop gambling despite mounting, serious and negative consequences.

8. Gambling leads to breaking the law to obtain gambling money or recover gambling losses.

9. Risking the loss of relationships or significant opportunities in order to maintain gambling habits.

10. Turning to family, friends, or a third party for financial assistance to bail them from gambling debts.

For most, gambling is a harmless form of entertainment. For 1% however, gambling is a serious problem. At least once a year, more than 80% of adults gamble.

Roadblocks:

- "I know gambling is interfering with my life, but I love gambling. I could be doing something worse."

- "Gambling isn't the real problem, lack of money is. If I had more money, no one would care about my gambling."

- "I don't need to stop gambling. I just need to manage and budget my finances better."

- "If everyone would just back off of me, sooner or later I'd get tired of gambling and stop."

- "My life would be so boring if I didn't gamble."

- "I've been gambling for too long. To quit completely is impossible."

Compulsive Gambling

Gamblers Anonymous offers the following questions to anyone who may have a gambling problem. These questions are provided to help the individual decide if he or she is a compulsive gambler and wants to stop gambling.

1. Do you ever lose time from work or school due to gambling?

2. Has gambling ever made your home life unhappy?

3. Has gambling affected your reputation?

4. Have you ever felt remorse after gambling?

5. Do you ever gamble to get money with which to pay debts or otherwise solve financial difficulties?

6. Does gambling cause a decrease in your ambition or efficiency?

7. After losing, do you feel you must return as soon as possible and win back your losses?

8. After a win do you have a strong urge to return and win more?

9. Do you often gamble until your last dollar is gone?

10. Do you ever borrow to finance your gambling?

11. Have you ever sold anything to finance gambling?

12. Were you reluctant to use "gambling money" for normal expenditures?

13. Does gambling make you careless of the welfare of yourself or your family?

14. Do you ever gamble longer than you had planned?

15. Have you ever gambled to escape worry or trouble?

16. Have you ever committed, or considered committing, an illegal act to finance gambling?

17. Does gambling cause you to have difficulty in sleeping?

18. Do arguments, disappointments, or frustrations create within you an urge to gamble?

19. Do you ever have an urge to celebrate any good fortune by a few hours of gambling?

20. Have you ever considered self-destruction or suicide as a result of your gambling?

Most compulsive gamblers will answer yes to at least seven of these questions.

Gambling Statistics

What is unique about the current gambling situation is the speed at which it has gone from an undercurrent in American society to high-profile, socially recognized activity.

- The gambling industry has grown tenfold in the U.S. since 1975.

- 47 states now have lotteries.

- 15 million people display some sign of gambling addiction.

- Two-thirds of the adult population placed some kind of bet last year.

- Gambling profits in casinos are more than $30 billion while lotteries are about $17 billion annually.

- "Players" with household incomes under $10,000 bet nearly three times as much on lotteries as those with incomes over $50,000.

- In 1973, state lotteries had $2 billion in sales. By 1997, the revenues reached $34 billion.

- Gambling among young people is on the increase: 42% of 14-year-olds, 49% of 15-year-olds, 63% of 16-year-olds, and 76% of 18-year-olds.

- There are now approximately 260 casinos on Indian reservations (in 31 states and with $6.7 billion in revenue).

- Internet gambling has nearly doubled every year since 1997. In 2001, it exceeded $2 billion.

- The Internet boasts 110 sport-related gambling sites.

- According to the American Psychological Association, the Internet could be as addictive as alcohol, drugs, and gambling.

- After casinos opened in Atlantic City, the total number of crimes within a thirty-mile radius increased 100%.

- The average debt incurred by a male pathological gambler in the U.S. is between $55,000 and $90,000 (it is $15,000 for female gamblers).

- The average rate of divorce for problem gamblers is nearly double that of non-gamblers.

- The suicide rate for pathological gamblers is twenty times higher than for non-gamblers (one in five attempts suicide).

- 65% of pathological gamblers commit crimes to support their gambling habit.

Change of Lifestyle

Learning how to recognize healthy choices can be one way to help you address gambling concerns.

Awareness:

Become familiar with your hot spots. If you have an urge to gamble, remove yourself from the situation immediately. Call someone you feel comfortable talking to and share what you are experiencing.

Finances:

Allow a spouse or someone you trust to be in charge of your money while you're working on your gambling problems. Block yourself from using credit cards, bank account access, or obtaining loans. Get someone to hold you accountable for setting these goals.

Keeping Busy:

Plan recreational time that doesn't involve gambling or maladaptive behaviors. Ask your family or friends about things they like to do. Try something new and positive.

Support Team:

Find out where gambling anonymous meetings are held. Let your gambling colleagues know you are trying to quit and ask them to support your effort by not involving you with gambling activities. Stay clear of gambling shacks, casinos, betting shops, and race tracks.

When you are ready, for advice or a treatment referral, call the National Council on Problem Gambling's <u>confidential</u> hotline at 1-800-522-4700.

Chapter 27 - Delli Dell's Story

PURPOSE:

Follow the dynamics of Delli Dell as he comes to terms with how his choices are affecting his behaviors and outcome.

GENERAL COMMENTS:

Optional strategies for facilitators.

1. Have participants read the story individually and then process it with the group.

2. Have participants go around the group table or circle and each participant read one paragraph and then process with the group.

3. Have participants separate into groups and have the chosen person read the story to the individual group. The individual groups discuss the story before coming back to the group as a whole and then process.

4. Facilitator reads the story to the group and then allows the group to process.

ACTIVITY:

Facilitator will have participants read Delli Dell's Story and process the events of his story.

176

A question for the provider:

Have you ever experienced confusion about your relationship in your life? _______________________________

What event happened? _______________________________

Do you still sometimes think about it? _______________________________

How do you feel now about the event? _______________________________

Did you filter it with values or fears? _______________________________

Values =

Responsibility

- Accept obligations
- Did the right thing in the situation/ or didn't repeat situation
- Accept accountabilities of your actions

Fears =

Avoid Responsibility

- Lack of positive thinking
- Lack of courage
- Lack of knowledge of what to do

177

Delli Dell's Story

Congratulations!

My family is bailing me out of jail . . . again. *Why don't I learn relapse?* For me, almost indubitably, it leads to recidivism (criminal behaviors). I know I shouldn't have gone out with my cousins that night. If I would have kept my butt at home like my wife asked me to I would not be facing this new DWI charge. But what bothers me the most is that I was doing well. I was attending my 12-step meetings, keeping in contact with my sponsor. I cannot explain what went wrong. My wife and I were getting along, my family trusted me, and I was even paying my bills on time. And now after three months of being clean and sober, and because of one crazy night, I am back in trouble with the courts again.

I am going to let you in on a little secret: *fear has been the foundation that stunts my growth.* The truth is, my growing seed has been delayed because of my fear of rejection and failure. As far back as I can remember, my fear has kept me from pursuing my goals in life and enjoying true peace inside myself. By the age of fifteen, I discovered alcohol and drugs and it became my way to suppress my fears. So as you may be able to tell right now, my thinking and behaviors are equal to a fifteen-year-old kid.

This is a real low point in my life, but it is also fearful for another reason: in the past when I have felt this low I have contemplated and even attempted suicide two times. When I get like this, I feel like no one understands the pain I'm experiencing. The worst part is, I don't send out many warning signals that say something is wrong and I continue to function as if everything is okay with me. I sincerely know my family and friends love me and I surely love them back. But when the pain is this unbearable, I just can't see it ever ending. Fortunately for me, the pain did end in the past, yet I'm here to tell you: at times the pain is very intense.

Even after all that happened to me, I am realizing I must move on from the red zone into recovery if I truly want to enjoy life to the fullest. The first step is to admit what's really going on with me, have the courage to change the things I can, and work with others who will assist me in reaching my goals.

My sponsor tells me that the way to make progress is to communicate my needs and wants because people are not mind readers. So my life can no longer be about excuses and alibis. I deserve love in my life and so does my family. After all that I have put my family through, it should be easy for me to start giving back. I realize it's not always going to be easy. But today I am taking on my responsibilities as my family quarterback. Communication is the key ingredient for healthy relationships.

For more than twenty years I have used drugs and alcohol to mask my fears. I now believe it's time to depend on my coping skills rather than my chemical dependency. I have come to believe my coping skills came before my chemical dependency. Now it may take a lot of work but my natural coping skills have never left me. I just need to go and rediscover them. However, things may not always go as I would like them to, but that's okay. That's life.

My wife and I won't always have the same view. That's okay. Sounds like life. However, she is the woman I love and I have made a personal, conscious effort to manage my anger and be patient with her and my children. My partner is more important to me than my anger, alcohol, and drug use.

Chapter 28 - Recidivism and Relapse

PURPOSE:

To reduce negative stress that leads to old behaviors by identifying warning signs.

GENERAL COMMENTS:

Recognizing warning signs can lower high-risk activities that lead to recidivism and relapse.

ACTIVITY:

1. Discuss Recidivism and Relapse as a group or with individual participants.

2. Ask participants if they have anything to add.

3. Allow participants to share their direct or indirect experiences with Recidivism and Relapse.

180

A question for the provider:

Notes

Have you ever been in a situation in your life where you could have stolen something? _______________________

What event happened? _______________________
____
____

Do you still sometimes think about it? _______________________
____
____

How do you feel now about the event? _______________________
____
____

Did you filter it with values or fears? _______________________
____
____

Values =
Responsibility

- Accept obligations
- Did the right thing in the situation/ or didn't repeat situation
- Accept accountabilities of your actions

Fears =
Avoid Responsibility

- Lack of positive thinking
- Lack of courage
- Lack of knowledge of what to do

181

Recidivism and Relapse

Recidivism - a tendency to slip back into a previous criminal behavior.

Criminal behaviors can start at an early age. Examples include:

- Hitting other children
- Shoplifting
- Jaywalking
- Destroying property

- Hurting animals
- Cheating
- Trespassing

What may be considered to be small criminal behaviors can have the potential which leads to larger criminal behaviors. Some examples include:

- Domestic violence / Assault / Battery
- Robbing / Embezzlement
- Reckless driving / DUI
- Arson / Vandalizing

- Hurting people
- Cheating (taxes, business, etc.)
- Breaking and Entrance

Absolutely no criminal behavior should go unaddressed.

Remember, the earlier a person begins to identify with what criminal behaviors are, the better chance of defusing recidivism.

Relapse - to revert to an earlier condition, after a partial or full recovery.

Research shows that first times DUI offenders have driven under the influence many times before getting caught. When a person drinks and drives, the odds of not getting caught are in their favor.

The number one leading cause of death for 16 to 24-year-old Americans is drunk driving. Drunk driving is the nation's most frequently committed violent crime. Under the influence, a person is ten times more likely to cause or be in a traumatic situation than when they are not under the influence.

To minimize your chance of Recidivism and Relapse, recognize these three pertinent behaviors:

1. High-risk thinking

2. High-risk feelings

3. High-risk situations

"The number one leading cause of death for 16 to 24-year-old Americans is drunk driving."

Chapter 29 - The Growing Seed

PURPOSE:

To improve understanding and self-awareness between adolescent and adult growth.

GENERAL COMMENTS:

Growing up at times can be mysterious and frightful, yet all adults experience it.

ACTIVITY:

1. Discuss The Growing Seed as a group or with individual participants.

2. Ask participants if they have anything to add.

3. Allow participants to share their direct or indirect experiences with The Growing Seed.

4. Fill in the blanks.

184

Notes

Have you ever made immature decisions as an adult in your life? ____

What event happened? ________________________________
____
____

Do you still sometimes think about it? ________________
____
____

How do you feel now about the event? ________________
____
____

Did you filter it with values or fears? ________________
____
____

Values =

Responsibility

- Accept obligations
- Did the right thing in the situation/ or didn't repeat situation
- Accept accountabilities of your actions

Fears =

Avoid Responsibility

- Lack of positive thinking
- Lack of courage
- Lack of knowledge of what to do

185

The Growing Seed

The Growing Seed Growth Chart							
Seed	Infant	Toddler	Little Kid	Big Kid	Pre-teen	Teen	Adult
*	0 to 1	2 to 3	4 to 7	8 to 10	11 to 12	13 to 17	18 +

As people grow, they should find themselves in an environment that calls for more responsibility.

Without proper guidance, the seed may find it difficult to adapt in a world of adults when they become one.

It is crucial that all parents understand the growing seed. As a seed moves closer to becoming an adult, the parent is ultimately responsible for them until the age of eighteen.

The growing map allows the parent to monitor their children's growth by placing proper responsibilities upon their children.

Group discussion: What responsibilities would you place on an:

Seed *

Infant 0 to 1

Toddler 2 to 3

Little kid 4 to 7

Big kid 8 to 10

Pre-teen 11 to 12

Teen 13 to 17

What are a few of the many responsibilities most adults are expected to do on a regular basis?

Think about it parents: it's very difficult to lead a seed into a healthy adult life if you have stopped growing yourself.

Remember a child thinks like a child and an adult thinks like an adult.

Quote of the day:

"Anytime you come upon a fifty-one-year-old man who continues to think and behave as he did when he was twenty-one years old, you've witnessed a man who has wasted thirty years of his life."

-Lendell L. Jones

Teaching our children how to grow is the most powerful gift any parent could give their children.

Chapter 30 - Suicide in the United States
A Cry for Help

PURPOSE:

To promote awareness of how suicide tragedies affect many families every year.

GENERAL COMMENTS:

About one million people worldwide take their own life each year.

ACTIVITY:

1. Discuss Suicide as a group or with individual participants.

2. Ask participants if they have anything to add.

3. Allow participants to share their direct or indirect experiences with Suicide and suicide attempts.

190

Have you ever contemplated suicide in your life? __________

What event happened? _________________________________

____

____

Do you still sometimes think about it? ____________________

____

____

How do you feel now about the event? ____________________

____

____

Did you filter it with values or fears? ____________________

____

____

Values =

Responsibility

- Accept obligations
- Did the right thing in the situation/ or didn't repeat situation
- Accept accountabilities of your actions

Fears =

Avoid Responsibility

- Lack of positive thinking
- Lack of courage
- Lack of knowledge of what to do

191

Suicide in the United States

Suicide is a common and increasing tragedy that affects many lives. Hundreds of thousands of people attempt or commit suicide every year. Elderly people are the most common age group to attempt or commit suicide. Between the age of 15 to 24, suicide is the third leading cause of death. If the person gets the proper help in time, suicide is usually preventable. By understanding the warning signs, you may someday help someone from committing suicide.

There may be many reasons a person thinks of committing suicide.

- Sometimes a person may feel very depressed and think suicide is their only escape.

- Mental illness and personality disorders are also reasons a person may attempt or commit suicide.

- Alcohol and drug use could also be a factor. While under the influence, the reasoning ability is reduced, and this can lead to an accidental or irrational decision to attempt or commit suicide.

- Sometimes family history plays a role. A person who has lost a loved one through suicide may also choose to attempt or commit suicide.

- People who have a low level of the brain chemical serotonin may be at higher risk of suicide.

- Sometimes people with chronic illnesses attempt or commit suicide. They may feel that ending their lives is better than suffering from their illness.

- Women are more likely to attempt suicide during a crisis. Men, however, are more likely to succeed in committing suicide during a crisis.

- Native Americans and Anglos have higher suicide rates than other groups.

- Married people have a lower suicide rate than those who are single, widowed, or divorced.

- Suicide is more common among people who are unemployed.

3 Common Myths about Suicide

1. Myth: Talking about suicide may give a person the idea.

Fact: People who are suicidal already have the idea. Discussing suicide can help prevent a person from acting on it.

2. Myth: People, who make unsuccessful suicide attempts, are only trying to seek attention.

Fact: Often, a suicide attempt is a way to get attention—it's the person reaching out for help. Dismissing the incident only makes matters worse. If the person doesn't get proper help, he or she may make a more serious suicide attempt next time.

3. Myth: Once people are suicidal, they can no longer be helped.

Fact: The crisis period sometimes lasts only for a limited time. However, a person can get help and improve. Remember, another crisis can occur. It's important to take each occurrence seriously and get the person the help they need.

Suicide Warning Signs:

- People may threaten to take their lives. They may say, "It's no use to live," or "Nothing really matters."

- They may make unexpected changes in their lives, or start giving their personal possessions away.

- They may start withdrawing from family and friends and appear depressed often.

- They may have a change in mood like going from sad to happy. Such a sudden mood change could mean they are relieved because their problems will soon end.

- They may experience changes in sexual, sleeping, or eating habits.

- People who have attempted suicide before may attempt suicide again.

Emotional Support:

- Show a person who is suicidal that you care by taking their feelings seriously.

- Listen to them and help them discuss their feelings. Explain to them that they can recover and professional help is available.

- Don't argue, challenge, reason, or try to analyze the suicidal person's motives.

- Help the person view their reasons to live and help them see that no problem is too big to solve.

When suspecting that someone is about to make a suicide attempt:

- Immediately get help. In an emergency, call 911. Do not leave the person alone until help arrives.

- Try to keep the person from using drugs and alcohol. Alcohol and drug use can impair a person's thinking.

- Become aware of your local suicide hotline, and become a volunteer at a crisis prevention center that will help those in need.

Remember: The more you know about suicide and the warning signs, the greater chance you have of helping someone in need.

Chapter 31 - Red Zone to Recovery

PURPOSE:

To recognize challenges that may become obstacles in one's life which can be a thin line between success and failure.

GENERAL COMMENTS:

Hard work and consistency are usually the ingredients for success.

ACTIVITY:

1. Discuss Red Zone to Recovery as a group or with individual participants.

2. Ask participants if they have anything to add

3. Allow participants to share their direct or indirect experiences with Red Zone to Recovery.

4. Fill in the blanks.

196

A question for the provider:

Notes

In your life, have you ever given up on something you believed in? _______________________________

What event happened? _______________________________
____
____

Do you still sometimes think about it? _______________________________
____
____

How do you feel now about the event? _______________________________
____
____

Did you filter it with values or fears? _______________________________
____
____

Values =

Responsibility

- Accept obligations
- Did the right thing in the situation/ or didn't repeat situation
- Accept accountabilities of your actions

Fears =

Avoid Responsibility

- Lack of positive thinking
- Lack of courage
- Lack of knowledge of what to do

197

Lendell L Jones

Red Zone to Recovery

Recovery is like football, as the map below will demonstrate. In the beginning, many people come out for the team. However, as time goes by and training becomes more intense, players began to drop out and go back to what is most comfortable. Well, the same is true for recovery. When a person first finds themselves in a tight spot or deals with a hard stressor, many times they go back to what has been comfortable. The map measures how many, out of a thousand, push forward.

Beginning

Pee Wee	Middle School	High School	College	Professional	Pro Bowl
1000	900	700	500	300	100
	1000	1000	1000	1000	1000

The same is true for recovery, although the map demonstrates an opposite pattern. With recovery, we can start with the same of amount of beginners; however, as the years go by, the chances of continuous recovery increase.

Beginning

Recovery	1 year	2 years	3 years	4 years	5 years
1000	100	300	500	700	900
	1000	1000	1000	1000	1000

Lendell L Jones

O.C. Original Counselor

Rules of Champions:

Champions give more.

Self-Discipline	Self-Control	Consistency	Identity	Work
Learn Rules	Manage Emotions	Accountable	Own Your Values	Task Focus
Practice	Be Noble	Confident	Respect Authority	Research
Attend Meetings	Develop Skills	honest	Integrity	Practice
Self Boundaries	Compassion	Keep Learning	Servant	Work Hard

Chapter 32 - How do you Communicate?

PURPOSE:

To strengthen relationships by understanding your way of communicating with others.

GENERAL COMMENTS:

There are many ways to communicate. Verbal communication is only one way to perform.

ACTIVITY:

1. Discuss as a group or with individual participants, How Do You Communicate?

2. Ask participants if they have anything to add.

3. Allow participants to share their direct or indirect experiences with How Do You Communicate?

4. Fill in the blanks.

200

A question for the provider:

Notes

Have you experienced having a hard time communicating with others in your life? _______________________

What event happened? _______________________

____

____

Do you still sometimes think about it?_______________________

____

____

How do you feel now about the event?_______________________

____

____

Did you filter it with values or fears? _______________________

____

____

Values =
Responsibility

- Accept obligations
- Did the right thing in the situation/ or didn't repeat situation
- Accept accountabilities of your actions

Fears =
Avoid Responsibility

- Lack of positive thinking
- Lack of courage
- Lack of knowledge of what to do

201

How Do You Communicate?

Today's exercise will be on communication. There are five scenarios and your position is to read them and apply the answer that best fits you.

Scenario 1

You and your partner are out for a Sunday drive when you both decided to go through a drive-through restaurant. After your partner completes their meal, they throw the trash out the window. How do you communicate this situation?

1. You stop or order the vehicle to be stopped and demand your partner go and retrieve the trash.

2. Call off your relationship because you refuse to be with a litterbug.

3. You continue with your drive and don't say anything about it.

4. (Other) ____

____

Scenario 2

Your parents are having a dinner to celebrate their twenty-fifth anniversary and you have been helping to plan this for months. Your partner clearly understands how important it is for both of you to attend this event. The dinner starts at 7:00 p.m. By 8:00 p.m. your partner has not arrived nor called to give reasons. At 8:35, your partner finally arrives. Do you?

1. Scream, yell, and become furious with your partner upon arrival.

2. Ignore your partner the rest of the night.

3. Believe in your heart your partner has a legitimate reason for not calling you and being late.

4. (Other) ____

____

Scenario 3

You are at one of the local malls with your partner when an ex-boyfriend/girlfriend approaches. The ex and your partner enter into a conversation of past events and catch up on what each other has been doing with their lives. Your partner at this point has not yet introduced you. What is your response to this?

1. Become angry and walk away.

2. Stand there while they continue their conversation.

3. Take the initiative and introduce yourself.

4. (Other) ____

____

Scenario 4

You love your partner very much. However, as of late, they have not been able to satisfy you romantically. Do you try to?

1. Avoid romantic situations with your partner.

2. Pretend you are being fulfilled and satisfied.

3. Let your partner know your likes and dislikes romantically.

4. (Other) ____

____

Scenario 5

You are driving your partner to the lake when your favorite song comes on the radio. While you are enjoying the music, your partner reaches over and changes the radio station. What do you do?

1. Tell your partner you like that song and for them to put it back.

2. Don't say anything but you're secretly upset with your partner.

3. Take the initiative and change the radio station back.

4. (Other) ____

____

Reminder: Most communication isn't verbal. People communicate in many ways and the way people communicate is their way of teaching others how to treat them.

Chapter 33 - Guest Speaker

PURPOSE:

To give participants a view of what life can be like when going through grief and loss.

GENERAL COMMENTS:

The speaker will share his/her story on how he/she experienced grief and loss.

ACTIVITY:

Ask questions and gather information about support group communities and resources.

Lendell L Jones

O.C. Original Counselor

A question for the provider:

Notes

Have you ever been in a situation where . . . ___________

____

____

____

What event happened? ___________________________

____

____

Do you still sometimes think about it?_______________

____

____

How do you feel now about the event?_______________

____

____

Did you filter it with values or fears? ________________

____

____

Values =

Responsibility

- Accept obligations
- Did the right thing in the situation/ or didn't repeat situation
- Accept accountabilities of your actions

Fears =

Avoid Responsibility

- Lack of positive thinking
- Lack of courage
- Lack of knowledge of what to do

205

Lendell L Jones

Chapter 34 - Coping Skills vs. Chemical Dependency

PURPOSE:

To identify life's stressors and develop skills to cope with them in a natural way.

GENERAL COMMENTS:

Natural coping skills allow one to identify true feelings and emotions.

ACTIVITY:

1. Discuss Coping Skills vs. Chemical Dependency as a group or with individual participants.

2. Ask participants if they have anything to add.

3. Allow participants to share their direct or indirect experiences with Coping Skills vs. Chemical Dependency.

4. Fill in the blanks.

206

A question for the provider:

 **Notes**

Have you had a hard time coping with a specific situation in your life? ______________________

What event happened? ______________________

____

____

Do you still sometimes think about it? ______________________

____

____

How do you feel now about the event? ______________________

____

____

Did you filter it with values or fears? ______________________

____

____

Values =

Responsibility

- Accept obligations
- Did the right thing in the situation/ or didn't repeat situation
- Accept accountabilities of your actions

Fears =

Avoid Responsibility

- Lack of positive thinking
- Lack of courage
- Lack of knowledge of what to do

207

Coping Skills vs. Chemical Dependency

Question: What came first, coping skills or chemical dependency?

Answer: Coping Skills came before Chemical Dependency

Natural   *Primary*

Coping skills are your natural ability to deal with the environment you were born into. Usually, coping skills are primary. You relied on them before you relied on chemicals.

At what age did you first use chemicals? ____

Do you realize that when you started relying on chemicals you stopped relying on your natural coping skills to handle stressors and joys in your life? Before chemical dependency, it didn't matter what the stressors were. Whether joyous or sad, you managed all feelings, naturally.

Natural Coping Skills lead to:

- Change of Lifestyle

- Joy

- Confidence

- Energy

- Compassion

- Serenity

Unnatural   *Secondary*

Chemical dependency came later, as a way to feel better about the environment you were born into. Chemical dependency is secondary. You usually begin to rely on them later in your life.

Was it: 9, 14, 17, 28, 34?

Whatever age it was, when you started relying on chemicals, your coping skills began to diminish. Natural coping skills do not go away; however, by relying on chemicals for a long period of time, a person can forget how to use their natural coping skills.

Unnatural Coping Skills lead to:

- Roadblocks

- Excessive Anger

- Low Self-esteem

- Low Motivation

- Selfishness

- Fear

One of the most dangerous things about using alcohol and drugs is: **Much of the time you experience euphoria (feels good).**

However, for some people, over time, that euphoria turns to dependency. Once a person reaches dependency, it's like swimming three hundred yards out in the ocean. It's easy to get way out there. In fact, you're out there before you know it. Yet, when they turn around and decide to swim back to shore, the journey is more difficult. Unfortunately, many people don't make it back from their journey of dependency. However determined, the swimmer who is willing to face the challenges in front of them has a great chance of making it back to shore.

Chapter 35 - Partners and Anger

PURPOSE:

To strengthen relationships by understanding and developing healthy boundaries.

GENERAL COMMENTS:

Deciding what is more valuable: being right in a relationship or building a healthy relationship.

ACTIVITY:

1. Discuss Partners and Anger as a group or with individual participants.

2. Ask participants if they have anything to add.

3. Allow participants to share their direct or indirect experiences with Partners and Anger.

4. Fill in the blanks.

210

A question for the provider:

Notes

Has your anger ever interfered with your relationships in your life? ____

What event happened? ______________________________
____
____

Do you still sometimes think about it?________________
____
____

How do you feel now about the event?________________
____
____

Did you filter it with values or fears? ______________
____
____

Values =
Responsibility

- Accept obligations
- Did the right thing in the situation/ or didn't repeat situation
- Accept accountabilities of your actions

Fears =
Avoid Responsibility

- Lack of positive thinking
- Lack of courage
- Lack of knowledge of what to do

211

Partners and Anger

When anger hurts, who really gets hurt?

Partner 1: .... children .... siblings .... parents __________ friends

Partner 2:................ children .... siblings .... parents __________ friends

HOW? ____

____

Behavior Patterns you have used to gain control over your partner's emotional, psychological, and physical state.

Emotional:_______________ anger .... manipulation __________ control

Psychological:___________ anger .... manipulation __________ control

Physical: _______________ anger .... manipulation __________ control

When anger is resolved with patience and love, who really benefits?

Partner 1: .... children .... siblings .... parents __________ friends

Partner 2:................ children .... siblings .... parents __________ friends

HOW? ____

____

Behavior Patterns of a healthy response to your partner's emotional, psychological, and physical state.

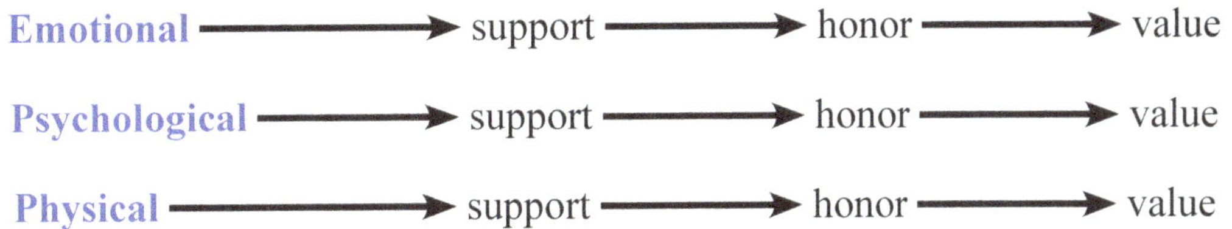

Emotional $\longrightarrow$ support $\longrightarrow$ honor $\longrightarrow$ value

Psychological $\longrightarrow$ support $\longrightarrow$ honor $\longrightarrow$ value

Physical $\longrightarrow$ support $\longrightarrow$ honor $\longrightarrow$ value

Anger is *"an emotional state that varies in intensity from mild irritation to intense fury and rage."* Give yourself permission to express it. The way we choose to express it determines the difference between negative and positive consequences.

Five tips to help release anger:

1. Accept anger in its natural form (a sensitive emotion).

2. Become aware of your hot spots and picture yourself handling those situations appropriately.

3. Remove yourself from the hot spot before you blow up. Revisit the situation later if needed.

4. Think, Think, and Think before reacting.

5. Memorize a little self-talk message you can use when your head is hot.

What causes anger?

Anger can be caused by both external and internal events. In general, it's the interpretation of the event that triggers the anger state. (Give examples of an external and an internal event.)

The two commons ways to express anger

Negative: Expressing angry feelings by lashing out at another person, threatening others, or passive-aggressive behaviors. Unexpressed anger is recognized as an unhealthy way to express anger. (Give examples.)

Positive: Expressing angry feelings in an assertive, non-aggressive manner is the healthiest way to express anger. (Give examples.)

Expressing anger in a negative way has the potential to lead to these outcomes:

- Hurt Feelings
- Low Self-esteem
- Guilt
- Regret
- Fear

- Isolation
- Alcohol/Drugs
- Unfaithfulness
- Jealousy
- Violence

Expressing anger in a positive way has the potential to lead to these outcomes:

- Contentment
- Confidence
- Assurance
- Comfort
- Relaxation

- Involvement
- Positive Activities
- Faithfulness
- Trustworthiness
- Peace

Remember: Anger is not our enemy once we learn the skills of managing it appropriately!

Love doesn't hurt! Out-of-control anger does!

Chapter 36 - Military Tactics

PURPOSE:

To identify what anger tactics are most often used and why these tactics have become comfortable.

GENERAL COMMENTS:

Anger is usually a secondary emotion trying to protect a primary feeling.

ACTIVITY:

1. Discuss Military Tactics as a group or with individual participants.

2. Ask participants if they have anything to add.

3. Allow participants to share their direct or indirect experiences with Military Tactics.

4. Fill in the blanks.

Lendell L Jones

O.C. Original Counselor

A question for the provider:

Notes

Have you ever had the opportunity to join the military in your life? _______________________________

What event happened? _______________________

____

____

Do you still sometimes think about it? _______________

____

____

How do you feel now about the event? _______________

____

____

Did you filter it with values or fears? _______________

____

____

Values =

Responsibility

- Accept obligations
- Did the right thing in the situation/ or didn't repeat situation
- Accept accountabilities of your actions

Fears =

Avoid Responsibility

- Lack of positive thinking
- Lack of courage
- Lack of knowledge of what to do

217

Lendell L Jones

Military Tactics

What is anger?

Answer: Anger is a natural emotion.

What causes anger?

Answer: Inability to control a person or situation. (Think about it: we don't become angry when things are going how we like.)

What is resentment?

Answer: Resentment is chronic anger that hangs around.

Anger is usually a secondary response/feeling. Most of the time, it is used as a protector of a vulnerable feeling.

Example: Anger protects:

- Fear
- Hurt
- Sadness
- Guilt
- Shame

Here are four examples of how anger is sometimes used. By becoming familiar with one's style of tactic, we can adopt effective ways of learning to recognize hot spots (things that lead to anger) and better manage anger before exploding.

The pattern of the four tactics has one thing in common: they all want to hit the bull's eye and at that particular time of the anger episode, they want the person or persons they are angry with to feel some of their pain.

(Counselors) Begin with Silent Sniper and give examples of the three behaviors the Silent Sniper demonstrate. When completed, ask the participants what the goal is. **Answer:** Hit the bull's eye. Do the same thing with the Soldier, Grenade, and Tank characters.

Remember it's okay to be angry, but it's not okay to hurt yourself, others, or animals, or to destroy things.

	Silent Sniper		Soldier

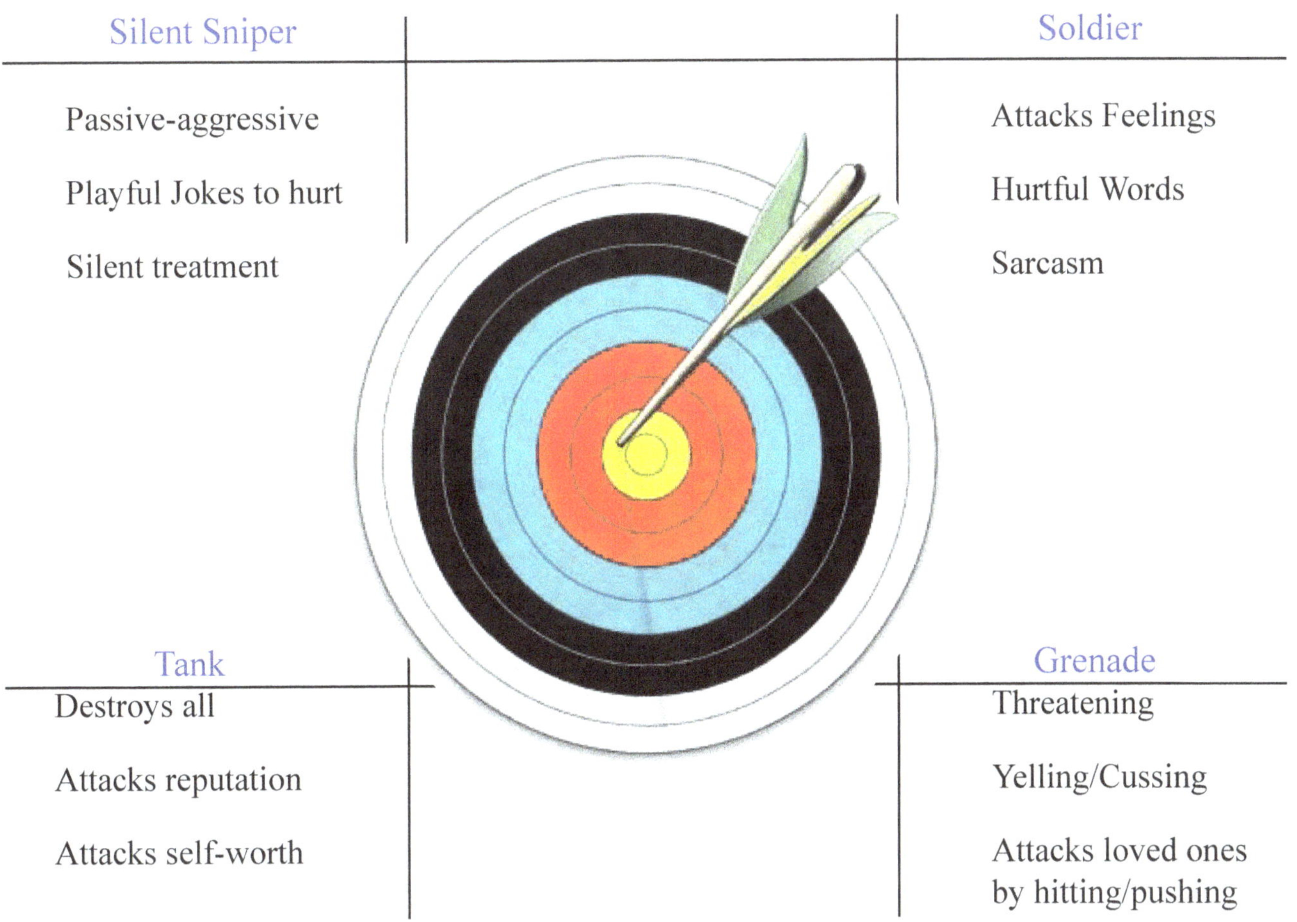

Silent Sniper

Passive-aggressive

Playful Jokes to hurt

Silent treatment

Soldier

Attacks Feelings

Hurtful Words

Sarcasm

Tank

Destroys all

Attacks reputation

Attacks self-worth

Grenade

Threatening

Yelling/Cussing

Attacks loved ones
by hitting/pushing

This is called Military Tactics. Most of these tactics have been used at one point or another.

Today, the focus is on which one of these tactics you are most familiar with and are most likely
to use: ____

Who are you most likely to use this tactic on? ____

____

Why that person? ____

____

After successfully using and hurting this person, what are your typical aftermath feelings as you
cool off? ____

____

Chapter 37 - Danger Zone

PURPOSE:

To increase awareness and knowledge on the dangers of pornography that can lead to many bad choices.

GENERAL COMMENTS:

We all agree that fantasies are important. It can have value in ways: to dream, believe, and push forward. But the level of fantasies can interfere with a person's emotional, mental, and physical health. It is allowing a person to make bad decisions and allowing for a decrease in self-esteem. Inform participants that this program was written many years ago and invite them to research updated statistics.

ACTIVITY:

1. Discuss The Danger Zone as a group or individually.

2. Ask the group or individual participants if they have anything to add.

3. Allow participants to share their direct or indirect experiences with Danger Zone.

A question for the provider:

Notes

Have you ever settled for sex when what you wanted was love in your life? _______________________________________

What event happened? _______________________________
____
____

Do you still sometimes think about it? _______________
____
____

How do you feel now about the event?_________________
____
____

Did you filter it with values or fears? _______________
____
____

Values =

Responsibility

- Accept obligations
- Did the right thing in the situation/ or didn't repeat situation
- Accept accountabilities of your actions

Fears =

Avoid Responsibility

- Lack of positive thinking
- Lack of courage
- Lack of knowledge of what to do

221

Danger Zone

Pornography is the new crack cocaine. It leads to addiction, misogyny, pedophilia, and low self-image, which leads to plastic surgeries and erectile dysfunction, according to clinicians and researchers.

Mary Anne Layden, co-director of the Sexual Trauma and Psychopathology Program at the University of Pennsylvania's Center for Cognitive Therapy, called porn the *"most concerning thing to psychological health that I know of existing today."*

> *"The Internet is a perfect drug-delivery system because you are anonymous, aroused, and there are role models that support these behaviors. This is a way to have a drug pumped into your house 24/7, free, and children know how to use it better than grown-ups – it's a perfect delivery system if we want to have a whole generation of young addicts who will never have the drug out of their minds."*

Pornography addicts have a more difficult time recovering from their addiction than cocaine and methamphetamine drug addicts, since drug users can get the drug out of their system, but pornographic images stay in the brain forever.

Jeffrey Satinover, a psychiatrist and advisor to the National Association for Research and Therapy of Homosexuality echoed Layden's concern about the internet and the somatic effects of pornography:

> *"Pornography really does, unlike other addictions, biologically cause direct release of the most perfect addictive substance," Satinover said. "That is, it causes masturbation, which causes release of the naturally occurring opioids. It does what heroin can't do, in effect."*

The internet is dangerous because it removes the inefficiency in the delivery of pornography, making porn much more ubiquitous than in the days when guys in trench coats would sell nudie postcards.

Many psychologists and most sexologists find the concepts of sex and pornography addiction problematic.

The Danger

- By the end of 2004, there were 420 million pages of pornography. (LaRue, Jan. "Obscenity and the First Amendment." Summit on Pornography. Rayburn House Office Building. Room 2322. May 19, 2005).

- The largest group of viewers of Internet porn are children between ages 12 and 17 (Family Safe Media, December 15, 2005).

- The Internet pornography industry generates 12 billion dollars in annual revenue -- larger than the combined annual revenues of ABC, NBC, and CBS (Family Safe Media, January 10, 2006).

- Pornographers "disguise" their sites with common brand names and misspellings designed to "entrap" people. (Ex: ESPN and Disney) (Source-surveillance study, March 1999.)

- Pornography in many forms is invading people's homes and is available 24 hours a day. In a short period of time, the Internet has become the most exploited instrument of perversion known to man.

- 51% of pastors say Internet pornography is a possible temptation. 37% say it is a current struggle. (Christianity Today, Leadership Survey, Dec 2001). 4 in 10 pastors have visited a porn website.

- Pornography is physically more addicting than cocaine and 'imprints' the mind with images. Overcoming pornography addiction takes years, and may affect you and everyone around you for the rest of your life.

- The average age of first exposure to Internet porn is 8 (Family Safe Media, December 15, 2005).

- A study by Focus on The Family, (March 2000) shows one in five adults, 20%, which is nearly 40 million people, have visited a sexually oriented website.

- Today's Christian Woman in 2003 found that one in six women (17%) including Christians, struggles with pornography addiction.

- Previously, if you wanted pornographic material you could buy a magazine, video, or visit some establishment. All of these put you at 'risk' of being found out. Now, with computers being used in private, unaccountable settings, people can find and view hard-core pornography right in their homes and offices. This can quickly escalate into an addiction with great harm brought to individuals, children, wives, and families.

- Five Stages to Addiction: Early exposure, addiction, escalation, desensitization, and acting out sexually. This addiction is committed with the mind and then, with the body, by acting out. It can destroy individuals, children, families, and marriages.

Commercial pornography sites:

- 74% display free teaser porn images on the homepage, often porn banner ads.

- 66% did not include a warning of adult content.

- 11% included such a warning but did not have sexually explicit content on the homepage.

- 25% prevented users from exiting the site (mousetrapping).

- Only 3% required adult verification (Child-Proofing on the World Wide Web: A Survey of Adult Webservers, 2001, Jurimetrics. National Research Council Report, 2002).

- According to the Florida Family Association, PornCrawler, their specialized software program, identified 20 U.S. companies that accounted for more than 70% of 297 million porn links on the Internet.

- According to Comscore Media Metrix, 71.9 million people visited adult sites in August 2005, reaching 42.7% of the Internet audience.

Prevention: Pornography addiction, and the destruction it causes, can be prevented by recognizing the danger and taking immediate action. You never know when temptation will strike. Protect yourself, your family, and your marriage.

For more information, please contact us at 1-877-479-1119 opt 3 or

resources@covenanteyes.com.

Chapter 38 - Wooly Bully

PURPOSE:

To increase awareness and knowledge on the dangers of bullying that can lead to many short and long-term effects in one's life.

GENERAL COMMENTS:

Bullying is a widespread problem and one of the hardest things about it is admitting that it might be happening to you.

ACTIVITY:

1. Discuss Wooly Bully as a group or individually.

2. Ask the group or individual participants if they have anything to add.

3. Allow participants to share their direct or indirect experiences with Wooly Bully.

226

A question for the provider:

Notes

Have you ever been a bully in your life? _____________

What event happened? _________________________

____

____

Do you still sometimes think about it?_____________

____

____

How do you feel now about the event?_____________

____

____

Did you filter it with values or fears? _____________

____

____

Values =

Responsibility

- Accept obligations
- Did the right thing in the situation/ or didn't repeat situation
- Accept accountabilities of your actions

Fears =

Avoid Responsibility

- Lack of positive thinking
- Lack of courage
- Lack of knowledge of what to do

227

Wooly Bully

Why does bullying happen?

There is no one clear reason for bullying, but a number of contributing factors might make it more likely to happen. Two of the main reasons people are bullied are because of appearance and social status. Bullies pick on the people they think don't fit in. How a person looks and how they act may make them a target. People who are perceived as shy or withdrawn are more susceptible to bullying or they may be targeted due to their race or religion.

<u>Bullying is no laughing matter</u>. Bullying is a problem that affects millions of people, and it has everyone worried, not just the people on its receiving end. Yet because parents, teachers, employers, loved ones, and friends don't always see it, they may not understand h o w extreme bullying can get.

For the victim who encounters a negative impact, there are no neat and tidy solutions. Bullying is when a person is picked on over and over again by an individual or group with more power, either in terms of physical strength or social standing.

Some bullies attack their targets physically, which can mean anything from shoving or tripping to punching or hitting, or even sexual assault. Others use psychological control or verbal insults to put themselves in charge. For example, people in popular groups or cliques often bully people they categorize as different by excluding them or gossiping about them (psychological bullying. They may also taunt or tease their targets (verbal bullying.

<u>Bullying is a form of abuse</u>. It comprises repeated acts over time that involve a real or perceived imbalance of power with the more powerful individual or group abusing those who are less powerful. The power imbalance may be social power and/or physical power. The victim of bullying is sometimes referred to as a target.

Bullying consists of three basic types of abuse: emotional, verbal, and physical. It typically involves subtle methods of coercion such as psychological manipulation. Bullying can be defined in many different ways. Some states have laws against it.

Types of Bullies

Sadistic, Narcissistic Bully:

This type lacks empathy for others and demonstrates low anxiety about consequences. They may appear to have high self-esteem but it is actually a brittle narcissism.

Imitative Bully:

This type may have low self-esteem or be depressed. They are influenced by the surrounding social climate. They may use whining or tattling or be manipulative.

Impulsive Bully:

This type is less likely to be part of a group and is more spontaneous and often appears more random. They may have difficulty restraining from their behaviors even when authorities are there to impose consequences. They also may be likely to be bullied.

Physical Bullies:

This type of bullying includes hitting or kicking the victim, or taking or damaging the victim's property. This is the least sophisticated type of bullying because it is so easy to identify.

Verbal Bullies:

This type of bully uses words to hurt or humiliate another person. Verbal bullying includes name-calling, insulting, making racist comments, and constant teasing. This type of bullying is the easiest to inflict on others. It is quick and to the point. It can occur in the least amount of time available when no one else is around and its effects can be more devastating in some ways than physical bullying because there are no visible scars. The lack of visible scars often leads people to think that the victim is exaggerating and the victim may not receive the support that they need as there is no visible trail for others to follow.

Stressed, Impulsive, or Unintentional Bully:

This type occurs when someone is under stress or an institution is undergoing confusing, disorienting changes. This is the easiest to redirect.

Cyber Bully:

This type includes hateful e-mails and cyberstalking. The bully will often spread rumors, untruths, and trusted information to hurt others.

Subordinate Bully:

This type is perpetrated by subordinates bullying their employer or students bullying their teacher.

Serial Bully:

This type repeatedly intimidates or harasses one individual after another. A victim is selected and bullied for an extended period of time.

Secondary Bully:

This type starts to react to bullying by imitating or joining in on the behavior. They usually imitate others.

Pair Bullies:
This type joins forces to intimidate others. The participation of the second individual empowers the other.

Gang Bullies:
This type gathers a number of followers. There may be a loud, highly visible leader. If they are a quieter sort, the role may be more insidious.

Pressure Bullying or Unwitting Bullying:
This type is where the stress of the moment causes behavior to deteriorate; the person becomes short-tempered, irritable, and may shout or swear at others. Everybody does this from time to time, but when the pressure is removed, behavior returns to normal, the person recognizes the inappropriateness of their behavior, makes amends, apologizes, and—crucially—learns from the experience so that the next time the situation arises, they are better able to deal with it. This is "normal" behavior.

Regulation Bullying:
This type forces their target to comply with rules, regulations, procedures, or laws regardless of the appropriateness, applicability, or necessity. Legal bullying—the bringing of a vexatious legal action to control and punish a person—is one of the worst forms of bullying.

Participant Bullying:
This type is where employees are bullied by those they serve. Often the participants perceive themselves to be right. Participant bullying can also be employees bullying their participants.

Corporate Bullying:
This type deems any employee suffering from stress as weak and inadequate while aggressively ignoring and denying the cause of stress.

Who gets bullied?

You can be anywhere, a female or a male, blue-collar or white-collar—bullying can happen to anyone.

What does bullying look like?

Workplace bullying might include getting ignored, put down, left out, talked about, or humiliated. Although bullying tends to be subtle, when males bully, it is often more aggressive or physical. With females, it might be more psychological.

Signs of Bullying:

- Being left out of events

- Peers leaving the area when you enter

- Ignoring your feelings and emotions

- Being given the "silent treatment"

- Not being given the praise you thought you deserved

- Being treated rudely or disrespectfully

- Refusal of help when you ask

- Spreading rumors about you that aren't true and that nobody denies

- Being given little or no feedback about your performance

- Others responding slowly to requests that are important to you

- Being yelled or shouted at

- Receiving put-downs about your intelligence or competence

- Your telephone calls or other communications are ignored

- Your contributions are ignored

- Someone interferes with or sabotages your work

- Being the recipient of mean pranks

- Being lied to

- Being treated rudely without a valid reason

- Being given bigger workloads or shorter deadlines than peers

- Being accused of making a mistake on purpose

- A peer throws a temper tantrum when you disagree with them

- Being put down in front of others

Illness can occur from long-term bullying:

- Stroke

- Heart Attack

- Chronic Fatigue Syndrome

- Anxiety

- Panic Attacks

- Clinical Depression

- Post Traumatic Stress Disorder (PTSD)

Useful tips to overcome bullying:

- Ignore the taunting and walk away. Calmly withdraw from the situation.

- Do not fight back nor should you allow yourself to be a doormat to be walked on. It will only worsen the problem.

- Place yourself where others can witness the bullying if possible.

- Avoid places where the bullies usually are.

- Walk in groups and hang out with people who have similar interests.

- Look out for other people being harassed. Report any bullying incident to the proper authority.

- Do not flaunt expensive things or money. These can be target items that encourage justifying their bully behaviors.

- BBe confident. Put your head up and walk with your shoulders straight. Bullies usually pick on people who appear scared, weak, and unsure of themselves.

Chapter 39: Race Around The World

PURPOSE:

To discuss the concept of racism and its effects.

GENERAL COMMENTS:

The intention of racism is to harm or hurt others. Racism is when we take our natural desire for familiarity too far and we start to look down on everyone who's not like us.

ACTIVITY:

1. Discuss the questions in the chapter as a group.

2. Ask questions. Add your thoughts.

3. Share your direct or indirect experiences with Racism.

234

A question for the provider:

Notes

Have you ever been a racist in your life? _______________

What event happened? _______________________________

____

____

Do you still sometimes think about it? _______________

____

____

How do you feel now about the event?_______________

____

____

Did you filter it with values or fears? _______________

____

____

Values =

Responsibility

- Accept obligations
- Did the right thing in the situation/ or didn't repeat situation
- Accept accountabilities of your actions

Fears =

Avoid Responsibility

- Lack of positive thinking
- Lack of courage
- Lack of knowledge of what to do

235

Lendell L Jones

Race Around the World . . .

This chapter is an open group discussion.

How has being a racist made your life better? _______________________

____

Does race really matter? _____________________________________

____

Let's pretend for a minute that you have a child. Now let's pretend your child gets hit by a drunk driver by someone who is a different race than you. Your child is dying. Would it make you feel any better if the drunk driver was the same race as you? _______________

____

____

Separated by class or income level

Let me introduce you to two people I know, Billionaire Jake and Trailer Park Mitch. Jake and Mitch are the same race. Do you think Billionaire Jake is going to offer his well-groomed daughter Lisa to marry Trailer Park Mitch's uneducated alcoholic son Bubba? I mean come on . . . They ARE the same race.

Does being of the same race bring everyone together? _______________

Values make the difference . . . not race.

Do you trust every one of your own race? _______________________

Is there some sort of guarantee that your spouse will not cheat with someone of your own race?

____

Are you willing to entrust your children with every one of your own race? _______________

____

In business, should all business deals be settled with a handshake and a person's word, just because they're the same race as you? ____

____

Back to the beginning . . .

People are different . . . and birds of a feather flock together. It's natural for people to want to be around other people who are similar. Racism is when we take that too far and we start to look down on everyone who's not like us. The intention of racism is to harm or hurt others.

Let's get back to that first question: How has being a racist made your life better? _________

____

____

____

Lendell L Jones

O.C. Original Counselor

Vapor 1 Treatment Plan

Participant Name: ____

Counselor Name: ____

Problem Areas

Problem Area #1: ____

____

Goal: ____

____

Objective: ____

____

Target Date to Complete: ______________________________________

Problem Area #2: ____

____

Goal: ____

____

Objective: ____

____

Target Date to Complete: ______________________________________

Problem Area #3: ____

____

Goal: ____

____

Objective: ____

____

Target Date to Complete: ____

Participant Strengths: ____

____

____

____

Possible Barriers While In Treatment: ____

____

____

____

Number of Sessions Attended: ____

Comments: ____

____

____

____

Participant Signature: _________________________________ Date: ___________

Counselor Signature: _________________________________ Date: ___________

DWI/DUI Level II Education – Curriculum

Participant _________________ Track_______ Signature _____________________________

Counselor _______________ __ Tile _________ Signature ___________________

This is an Impaired Driver Education Program for persons who have been convicted of driving while their blood alcohol level went beyond legal limits or while they were under the influence of a drug or alcohol that impaired their normal ability in the State of _____________________.

A. Intervention

    1. Modality: Outpatient Services

    2. Method: Educational

    3. Placement Criteria: Outpatient

    4. GAF: _______

    5. Track _______ Hours _______

    6. Class Duration: 2 Hours

B. Treatment Objectives: Recognition and Acceptance

Cross-reference and complete 12 Lessons in the VAPOR 1

Education Curriculum Manual to complete the following objectives.

 Lendell L Jones   O.C. Original Counselor

1. Topic: 12 Steps of Growth

   Lesson Time: 2 hours

   Completion Date: _________Counselor_____________________Agency_________________

2. Topic: Community Tragedies

   Lesson Time: 2 hours

   Completion Date: _________Counselor_____________________Agency_________________

3. Topic: 12 Choices in Life

   Lesson Time: 2 hours

   Completion Date: _________Counselor_____________________Agency_________________

4. Topic: Delli Dell's Story

   Lesson Time: 2 hours

   Completion Date: _________Counselor_____________________Agency_________________

5. Topic: Model of Locus of Control

   Lesson Time: 2 hours

   Completion Date: _________Counselor_____________________Agency_________________

6. Topic: Domestic Violence

   Lesson Time: 2 hours

   Completion Date: _________Counselor_____________________Agency_________________

7. Topic: Impaired Drivers

   Lesson Time: 2 hours

   Completion Date: _________Counselor_____________________Agency_________________

8. Topic: The Body and Alcohol

    Lesson Time: 2 hours

    Completion Date: _________Counselor_________________ Agency_______________

9. Topic: Driver's Impairment

    Lesson Time: 2 hours

    Completion Date: _________Counselor_________________ Agency_______________

10. Topic: Guess Speaker

    Lesson Time: 2 hours

    Completion Date: _________Counselor_________________ Agency_______________

11. Topic: Drugs and the Consequences

    Lesson Time: 2 hours

    Completion Date: _________Counselor_________________ Agency_______________

12. Topic: Building Self-Esteem

    Lesson Time: 2 hours

    Completion Date: _________Counselor_________________ Agency_______________

13. Topic: How to build Self-Esteem

    Lesson Time: 2 hours

    Completion Date: _________Counselor_________________ Agency_______________

14. Topic: Level I, II, and III, the Power of Change

    Lesson Time: 2 hours

    Completion Date: _________Counselor_________________ Agency_______________

15. Topic: Delli Dell's Story II

    Lesson Time: 2 hours

    Completion Date: _________Counselor_____________________ Agency_____________

16. Topic: 1st and Goal

    Lesson Time: 2 hours

    Completion Date: _________Counselor_____________________ Agency_____________

17. Topic: Peaceful Fighting Amongst Partners

    Lesson Time: 2 hours

    Completion Date: _________Counselor_____________________ Agency_____________

18. Topic: Tools for Parents

    Lesson Time: 2 hours

    Completion Date: _________Counselor_____________________ Agency_____________

19. Topic: Three Commonly Used Parenting Skills

    Lesson Time: 2 hours

    Completion Date: _________Counselor_____________________ Agency_____________

20. Topic: Tips on Parenting

    Lesson Time: 2 hours

    Completion Date: _________Counselor_____________________ Agency_____________

21. Topic: Quarterbacking the Family

    Lesson Time: 2 hours

    Completion Date: _________Counselor_____________________ Agency_____________

22. Topic: Living With a Disability

       Lesson Time: 2 hours

       Completion Date: __________ Counselor____________________ Agency_____________

23. Topic: Guess Speaker

       Lesson Time: 2 hours

       Completion Date: __________ Counselor____________________ Agency_____________

24. Topic: Healthy Relationships

       Lesson Time: 2 hours

       Completion Date: __________ Counselor____________________ Agency_____________

25. Topic: Praising Relationships

       Lesson Time: 2 hours

       Completion Date: __________ Counselor____________________ Agency_____________

26. Topic: Gambling

       Lesson Time: 2 hours

       Completion Date: __________ Counselor____________________ Agency_____________

27. Topic: Delli Dell's Story III

       Lesson Time: 2 hours

       Completion Date: __________ Counselor____________________ Agency_____________

28. Topic: Recidivism and Relapse

       Lesson Time: 2 hours

       Completion Date: __________ Counselor____________________ Agency_____________

29. Topic: The Growing Seed

    Lesson Time: 2 hours

    Completion Date: _________Counselor__________________ Agency____________

30. Topic: Suicide

    Lesson Time: 2 hours

    Completion Date: _________Counselor__________________ Agency____________

31. Topic: Red Zone to Recovery

    Lesson Time: 2 hours

    Completion Date: _________Counselor__________________ Agency____________

32. Topic: How Do You Communicate

    Lesson Time: 2 hours

    Completion Date: _________Counselor__________________ Agency____________

33. Topic: Guess Speaker

    Lesson Time: 2 hours

    Completion Date: _________Counselor__________________ Agency____________

34. Topic: Coping Skills vs. Chemical Dependency

    Lesson Time: 2 hours

    Completion Date: _________Counselor__________________ Agency____________

35. Topic: Partners and Anger

    Lesson Time: 2 hours

    Completion Date: _________Counselor__________________ Agency____________

36. Topic: Military Tactics

      Lesson Time: 2 hours

      Completion Date: _________ Counselor___________________ Agency_____________

37. Topic: Danger Zone

      Lesson Time: 2 hours

      Completion Date: _________ Counselor___________________ Agency_____________

38. Topic: Wooly Bully

      Lesson Time: 2 hours

      Completion Date: _________ Counselor___________________ Agency_____________

39. Topic: Race Around The World

      Lesson Time: 2 hours

      Completion Date: _________ Counselor___________________ Agency_____________

C. Termination of Services Date:___________________________________

Daily Affirmations

- I am capable of change.

- I am a child of God.

- Today I will take a risk with someone I trust.

- I am willing to accept love.

- I will let go of the past and let my wounds heal.

- I am not alone; I am one with God and the Universe.

- Today I will let someone's compliment nurture me.

- I am a precious and worthwhile person.

- I forgive myself for hurting myself and others.

- Today I will act in a way I would admire in someone else.

- I am beautiful inside and out.

- I forgive myself for letting others hurt me.

- I deserve to be loved by myself and others.

- I love myself unconditionally.

- I deserve love, peace, prosperity, and serenity.

- I am whole and good.

- I am learning my purpose more and more as I "Let Go and Let God."

- I will open my eyes to the goodness in others.

- My Higher Power guides me on my path today.

- I will meet new opportunities without fear.

- I am worthy of positive change in my life.

- I create my own happiness.

- Today I am on my spiritual path to recovery.

- I am learning to flow with the current of life.

- I take charge of my life today.

- Today I choose to be free of resentments.

- I feel good about my life today.

- Today I take responsibility for my mistakes.

- Today I silence old negative messages and replace them with happy thoughts.

- I am learning to receive good things in my life.

- Today I will make wise choices and use good judgment.

- Wonderful choices are available to me today.

- Today I can hold my head up and walk tall.

- My Higher Power guides me on my path today.

Specialized Counseling Sessions

Date   Topic   Counselor Name

__12/13__ sweat lodge_______________________________ Lendell Jones______

_______ _____________________________________ ___________________

_______ _____________________________________ ___________________

_______ _____________________________________ ___________________

_______ _____________________________________ ___________________

_______ _____________________________________ ___________________

Individual Counseling Sessions

Agency: ___*(Your Counseling Agency Name goes here)*______

Date   Topic   Counselor Name

12/13 FAMILY STRENGTHS______________________ Lendell Jones______

_______ _____________________________________ ___________________

_______ _____________________________________ ___________________

_______ _____________________________________ ___________________

_______ _____________________________________ ___________________

_______ _____________________________________ ___________________

This is a PARTIAL SAMPLE ONLY of the sheet in the participant workbook. The participant form may take an entire page or more.

12-Step Meetings

Agency: *(Your Counseling Agency Name goes here)*

Date   Time / Agency   Chairperson

12/13 11 am to 12 pm / Mission Impossible Couns Lendell Jones

This is a PARTIAL SAMPLE ONLY of the sheet in the participant workbook. The participant form may take an entire page or more.

Community Service

Agency: *(Your Counseling Agency Name goes here)*

Date   Time   Supervisor

12/13 11 am to 12 pm   Lendell Jones

Other Providers Contacted

Date	Agency / (Topic optional)	Contact Name
12/13	Agency XYZ, talked about housing	Lendell Jones

Job Search & Interview Log

Date	Company	Position Applied For
12/13	Smiths Grocery Store	Cashier

This is a PARTIAL SAMPLE ONLY of the sheet in the participant workbook. The participant form may take an entire page or more.

Feeling Journal

Date   Today I feel...

12/13   Today I feel really great. It was the first day in a long time I went without having a drink. It's a really awesome feeling to know I'm not being controlled by the alcohol.

12/14   I made it through the weekend... but I feel like crap.

This is a PARTIAL SAMPLE ONLY of the sheet in the participant workbook. The participant form may take an entire page or more.

Exercise Log

Date   Hours   Activity

12/13   2 hours   I walked 4 miles.

Children Activity & Interaction Log

Date	Time	Event
12/13	1 hour	I went swimming with my kids.

Spiritual Contact log

Date	Time	Event
12/13	10 to 11 am	I went to church.

Lendell L Jones

O.C. Original Counselor

This is a PARTIAL SAMPLE ONLY of the sheet in the participant workbook. The participant form may take an entire page or more.

Breath Alcohol Concentration Log

Date	Time	Result	Participant	Staff
12/13	3 pm	BAC level: .000	Delli Dell	Lendell Jones
		BAC level:		
		BAC level:		
		BAC level:		
		BAC level:		
		BAC level:		
		BAC level:		
		BAC level:		

This is a PARTIAL SAMPLE ONLY of the sheet in the participant workbook. The participant form may take an entire page or more.

Urine Analysis log

Date	Time	Result	Participant	Staff
12/13	1:15 pm	Negative / (Positive)	Delli Dell	Lendell Jones
		Positive for: cocaine		
		Negative / Positive		
		Positive for:		
		Negative / Positive		
		Positive for:		
		Negative / Positive		
		Positive for:		

Drunk Driving Laws in New Mexico

New Mexico's drunk driving law makes it illegal to operate a motor vehicle if your blood alcohol concentration (BAC) is .08 percent or above. The .08 limit is the standard measurement for the "impaired" driver in all states. The punishment, however, is not the same in all states. New Mexico has strict laws and penalties for drunk driving and even your first offense will be expensive (See Penalties). In addition to the .08 limit, New Mexico has lower limits for commercial drivers and drivers under the age of 21.

Penalties For Drunk Driving in New Mexico:

First Conviction (new)

- Jail – Up to 90 Days

- License Suspension – Up to 1 Year

- Ignition Interlock – 1 Year

- DWI School

- Alcohol Evaluation

- Community Service

- Treatment – (Possible)

Second Conviction

- Jail – Minimum 96 Hours up to 364 Days

- Fine – Minimum $500 up to $1,000

- License Suspension – 2 Years

- Ignition Interlock – 2 Years

- Alcohol Evaluation

- Community Service

- Treatment

- Probation – Up to 5 Years

Laws - *Consult your state for its specific laws, current laws, or changes.*

Third Conviction

- Jail – Minimum 30 days up to 364 Days

- Fine – Minimum $750 up to $1,000

- License Suspension – 3 Years

- Ignition Interlock – 3 Years

- Alcohol Evaluation

- Community Service

- Treatment

- Probation – Up to 5 Years

Fourth Conviction

- Felony Offense

- Prison – Minimum 6 Months up to 18 Months

- Fine – Minimum Up to $5,000

- License Suspension – Lifetime (With 5-Year Review)

- Ignition Interlock – Lifetime (After 5-Year Review)

- Alcohol Evaluation

- Treatment

Fifth Conviction

- Felony Offense

- Prison – Minimum 1 Year up to 2 Years

- Fine – Minimum Up to $5,000

- License Suspension – Lifetime (With 5-Year Review)

- Ignition Interlock – Lifetime (After 5-Year Review)

- Alcohol Evaluation

- Treatment

Drunk Driving Laws in Kansas

The drunk driving laws in Kansas prohibit driving with a blood alcohol concentration (BAC) of .08 percent or above. The limits are lower for drivers of commercial vehicles and minors. The .08 limit is the standard measurement used across the United States for the "impaired" driver. The Kansas law extends to alcohol, drugs, or both. If you are driving with a child under the age of 14 in your vehicle when you commit a DUI, your punishment will be extended by one additional month of imprisonment.

Penalties For Drunk Driving in Kansas

First Conviction

- Jail – 48 Hours Mandatory Minimum, or

- Community Service – 100 Hours

- Fine – From $500 to $1,000

- License Suspension – 30 Days

- License Restriction – 330 Days Following Suspension

- Vehicle Impound – Up to 1 Year Possible

- Court-Ordered Treatment Program Possible

Second Conviction

- Jail – From 90 Days to 1 Year

- Fine – From $1,000 to $1,500

- License Suspension – 1 Year

- Ignition Interlock Device – Required 1 Year after Suspension

- Vehicle Impound – Up to 1 Year Possible

- Complete Court-Ordered Treatment Program

Laws - *Consult your state for its specific laws, current laws, or changes.*

Third Conviction

- Felony Offense

- Jail – From 90 Days to 1 Year

- 72 Consecutive Hours Must be Served Prior to Work Release

- Fine – From $1,500 to $2,500

- License Suspension – 1 Year

- Ignition Interlock Device – Required 1 Year after Suspension

- Vehicle Impound – Up to 1 Year Possible

- Complete Court-Ordered Treatment Program

Fourth and Subsequent Conviction

- Felony Offense

- Jail – From 180 Days Minimum to 1 Year

- 144 Consecutive Hours Must Be Served Prior to Work Release

- Kansas Department of Corrections Post-Release Supervision for 1 Year

- Fine – $2,500 Minimum

- License Suspension – 1 Year

- Ignition Interlock Device – Required 1 Year after Suspension

- Vehicle Impound – Up to 1 Year Possible

- Complete Court-Ordered Treatment Program

Drunk Driving Laws in Colorado

The following driving actions are illegal in the State of Colorado:

- Under 21 – A blood alcohol content level (BAC) of .02 and less than .08

- Under 21 – In possession of alcohol

- Driving with a BAC of .05–.07 (Driving while Impaired)

- Driving with a BAC of .08 or above (Driving Under the Influence)

- Driving under the influence of Alcohol or Drugs or Both (DWAI)

Penalties For Drunk Driving in Colorado:

First DUI Conviction

Blood Alcohol Content .08 or Above

Fist DUI
- Jail – From 5 Days to 1 Year

- Fine - From $600 - $1,000

- License Suspension – 9 Months

- License Points – 12

- Public Service – From 48 to 96 Hours

- Jail may be suspended in lieu of Alcohol Treatment Program

- First DWAI Conviction

- Blood Alcohol Content of .05 But Less Than .08

Fist DWAI
- Jail – From 48 Hours to 180 Days

- Fine – From $200 to $500

- License Suspension – None

- License Points – 8

 Laws - *Consult your state for its specific laws, current laws, or changes.*

- Public Service – From 24 to 48 Hours

Second DUI Conviction

Blood Alcohol Content .08 or Above

- Jail – From 90 Days to 1 Year

- Fine – From $1,000 to $1,500

- License Suspension – 1 Year

- Ignition Interlock Device Prior to License Reinstatement*

- License Points – 12

- Public Service – From 60 to 120 Hours

- *If within 5 Years of Previous DUI

Second DWAI Conviction

- Blood Alcohol Content of .05 But Less Than .08

- Jail – From 90 Days to 1 Year

- Fine – From $1,000 to $1,500

- License Suspension – 1 Year

- License Points – 12

- Public Service – From 60 to 120 Hours

Third DUI Conviction

Blood Alcohol Content .08 or Above

- Jail – From 70 Days to 1 Year

- Fine – From $900 to $1,500

- License Suspension – 2 Years

- Ignition Interlock Device Prior to License Reinstatement

- License Points – 12

- Public Service – From 56 to 112 Hours

Third DWAI Conviction
- Blood Alcohol Content of .05 But Less Than .08

- Jail – From 45 Days to 1 Year

- Fine – From $600 to $1,000

- License Suspension – 2 Years

- License Points – 8

- Public Service – From 48 to 96 Hours

DWAI With Previous DUI Conviction
- Jail – From 60 Days to 1 Year

- Fine – From $800 to $1,200

- Public Service – From 52 to 104 Hours

DUI With Previous DWAI
- Jail – From 70 Days to 1 Year

- Fine – From $900 to $1,500

- Public Service – From 56 to 112 Hours

Laws - *Consult your state for its specific laws, current laws, or changes.*

SUCCESSFUL COMPLETION
LET IT BE KNOWN THAT
(NAME)
IS BEING RECOGNIZED THIS DAY
WITH THIS CERTIFICATE AS HAVING
SUCCESSFULLY COMPLED THE
VAPOR 1 EDUCATION
PROGRAM.
DATE
COUNSELOR'S NAME
COUNSELING AGENCY
HOURS

VAPOR 1 - PARTICIPANT PROGRESS SURVEY

Name: _________________________________ Agency: _____________________________ Date: __________

You are asked to answer the following questions as to your involvement in this program.

1. I understand how my thinking can lead to behaviors. .... Yes __ No__ Not sure__

2. I have a recidivism prevention plan... Yes__ No__ Not sure__

3. I have a relapse prevention plan. .... Yes__ No__ Not sure__

4. I understand how my thinking and behaviors affect others. .... Yes__ No__ Not sure__

5. I have a good understanding of my alcohol and drug pattern....... Yes__ No__ Not sure__

6. I paid attention and listened in class. .... Yes__ No__ Not sure__

7. I will use the information I learned in class. .... Yes__ No__ Not sure_

8. I took part in the group discussions. .... Yes__ No__ Not sure__

9. I found it easy to follow along with the topics. .... Yes__ No__ Not sure__

10. I had a positive attitude while in the program. .... Yes__ No__ Not sure__

11. I think the worksheets were helpful... Yes__ No__ Not sure__

12. I have made progress toward a positive change of lifestyle......... Yes__ No__ Not sure__

13. I was open and honest with my peers. .... Yes __ No__ Not sure__

14. I was open and honest with my counselor during
    individual sessions. .... Yes__ No__ Not sure__

15. I think the staff and counselors were knowledgeable about
    addiction and change behaviors.. Yes__ No__ Not sure__

16. I think this program is good and I will recommend it to
    others.. Yes__ No__ Not sure__

17. My overall rating of this program.. Good__ Fair__ Poor__